Digital Branding

Fourth Edition

Digital Branding

How to Successfully Build and Measure a Brand Online

Daniel Rowles

> **Publisher's note**
>
> Every possible effort has been made to ensure that the information contained in this book is accurate at the time of going to press, and the publishers and authors cannot accept responsibility for any errors or omissions, however caused. No responsibility for loss or damage occasioned to any person acting, or refraining from action, as a result of the material in this publication can be accepted by the editor, the publisher or the author.

First published in Great Britain and the United States in 2025 by Kogan Page Limited

Apart from any fair dealing for the purposes of research or private study, or criticism or review, as permitted under the Copyright, Designs and Patents Act 1988, this publication may only be reproduced, stored or transmitted, in any form or by any means, with the prior permission in writing of the publishers, or in the case of reprographic reproduction in accordance with the terms and licences issued by the CLA. Enquiries concerning reproduction outside these terms should be sent to the publishers at the undermentioned addresses:

2nd Floor, 45 Gee Street
London
EC1V 3RS
United Kingdom

c/o Martin P Hill Consulting
122 W 27th St, 10th Floor
New York, NY 10001
USA

www.koganpage.com

Kogan Page books are printed on paper from sustainable forests.

© Daniel Rowles, 2014, 2018, 2022, 2025

The right of Daniel Rowles to be identified as the author of this work has been asserted by them in accordance with the Copyright, Designs and Patents Act 1988.

ISBNs
Hardback   978 1 3986 1844 2
Paperback 978 1 3986 1842 8
Ebook   978 1 3986 1843 5

British Library Cataloguing-in-Publication Data

A CIP record for this book is available from the British Library.

Library of Congress Control Number

2022056825

Typeset by Integra Software Services, Pondicherry
Print production managed by Jellyfish
Printed and bound by CPI Group (UK) Ltd, Croydon CR0 4YY

*To my dad. Thanks for everything.
Except those horse racing tips…*

CONTENTS

List of figures and tables xii
Foreword by Chris Daly xv
Acknowledgements xvi

Introduction 1

PART ONE Digital branding in perspective

01 **What digital branding really means** 7
How digital has changed branding 7
AI and branding 8
Global soapbox 9
Social media fail 10
Traditional brand metrics 10
Sum of all experiences 11
Clarifying touchpoints 11
The role of digital transformation 12

02 **Focusing on value** 16
Bridging the gap 16
Value proposition 17
It all comes down to content 20

03 **Considering the user journey** 26
Multichannel marketing 26
User journey examples 26
Content marketing 29
The stages of the user journey 31
Content mapping 33
Value proposition and user journey 34
Mapping the user journey 34

04 Objectives and authenticity 43
Branding for differentiation 44
Authenticity 45
Authentic value proposition 46
Authenticity, AI and deepfakes 48

PART TWO The digital toolkit

05 Social media 51
Social is personal 51
User journey and value proposition 52
Content and engagement 52
Generative AI and content 52
Mobile social media experience 53
Informing your social media approach 54
Social media monitoring and listening tools 56
Analytics 59
Real-world integration 60
Effectively implementing a social media policy 60
Culture and process 61
How to avoid a social media disaster 62
Social media crisis management plan 69
Outreach, engagement and ego 71
Social media conclusions 76

06 Search 78
Enter the drumming gorilla 78
Search engine optimization 81
AI content and SEO 83
EEAT 83
Keyword search for SEO 84
On-page optimization 88
Link building 93
Social signals 94
User behaviour 94
Measuring link authority 95
SEO summary 96
Paid search 97

PPC considerations 101
SEO and PPC working together 103
Search conclusions 104

07 Mobile 105
Technology for the sake of technology 105
AI everywhere 106
User journey and context 106
Local intent 107
Integrated devices 107
The technology distraction 108
Mobile compatible is not mobile optimized 108
Technology challenges 109
Audience segmentation 110
Frictionless technology 110
Mobile sites and responsive design 110
Start with the fundamentals 111
Mobile apps 113
Mobile conclusions 114

08 Online advertising 115
Advertising objectives 116
Ad networks versus media owners 117
Targeting options 118
Creative options 119
Ad reporting and analytics 119
Online advertising conclusions 120

09 Email marketing 125
Focusing on the user 125
Email isn't exciting 125
Ease of iteration 127
AI tools and email 127
Focusing on relevance 129
Email and the user journey 129
Going beyond last click 130
Selecting an email service provider 132
Gaining opt-ins and building a list 133
List segmentation 135

Open rates and click-through rates 136
Email design 137
Email templates 139
Sending and testing 141
Dynamic content generation and rules 142
Email marketing conclusions 144

10 CRM and marketing automation 151
Definitions and practicalities 151
Single customer view and bringing data together 152
CRM and ESP integration 154
CRM and AI chatbots 156
Advanced personalization and triggering 157
Marketing automation 157
The lead nurturing process 158
Automation scoring 158
More advanced automation options 161
Testing, learning and adjusting 161
A warning on marketing automation 162
CRM and automation conclusions 162

11 From integration to transmedia campaigns 164
Integration 164
Multichannel marketing is dead 164
Omni-channel marketing 165
Transmedia storytelling 166
Self-optimizing campaigns 167
Integration to transmedia conclusions 167

PART THREE Digital brand strategy and measurement

12 Measuring digital branding 173
Defining brand value and valuation 173
Understand the value of every marketing activity 173
For perfection we need a mind-reading device 174
Digital shot itself in the foot 174
Moving to a cookieless world 175
TV has culture, digital doesn't 176

Filling the gaps 176
Benchmarked social measures 177
Measurement comes in many forms 179

13   Primaries and indicators 182
Beyond the last click 182
Digital branding dashboards 184

14   The role of analytics 185
Introduction to Google Analytics 4 185
Setting up analytics 187
Core reports 188
Attribution modelling 194
Tracking code 195
Dashboards and analytics 196
Analytics conclusions 197

15   Bridging the gaps 198
Gap correlation 198
Keeping it simple – and the danger of selecting the wrong primaries 199
Bring in offline channels and experiences 200
Offline indicators 201
A word on contribution 203
Seeing it in action 203

16   The importance of asking questions 207
Confirming not predicting 207
Sum of experiences 207
Checking my dashboard 208
No one said it was going to be easy 209

Conclusions 210

References and further reading 212
Index 215

LIST OF FIGURES AND TABLES

Figures

Figure 2.1 Aligned business and user objectives create value 17
Figure 2.2 Digital branding bridges the gap between business objectives and target audience objectives 17
Figure 3.1 The sales funnel 32
Figure 3.2 Avinash Kaushik's See, Think, Do, Care framework 32
Figure 3.3 The Movement Formula 37
Figure 5.1 Google Trends allows us to see volumes of searches for a particular phrase over time. This chart shows searches for the word 'jobs' 55
Figure 5.2 Comparing words in Google Trends 55
Figure 5.3 An example of the many social analysis tools out there and one of my favourites, SparkToro.com, looking at influential social accounts around the topic of branding 58
Figure 5.4 Word cloud of phrases mentioned online connected to social media disasters 60
Figure 5.5 Words used in association with social media disasters 61
Figure 5.6 Peaks in interest caused by new articles being published giving advice on the topic 62
Figure 5.7 Building a query for social media listening 65
Figure 5.8 Email alerts for topics that are growing quickly (screenshot of Brandwatch's 'Signals' system) 66
Figure 5.9 Upfluence is a social media influence scoring platform 72
Figure 6.1 Searches in Google for 'drumming gorilla' 79
Figure 6.2 Searches in Google for 'drumming gorilla' and 'cadburys' 80
Figure 6.3 Keyword volumes using Keywords Everywhere 87
Figure 6.4 Google Trends comparing search terms 88
Figure 6.5 The key elements of the page involved in SEO 90
Figure 6.6 The page title is the main line of the search result in Google 90

List of figures and tables

Figure 6.7	The excellent Link Explorer from Moz 96
Figure 6.8	Paid search in action in Google 98
Figure 7.1	A great example of responsive design in practice, showing the Target Internet website (http://www.targetinternet.com) – Figure 7.1a as the full-width version, and Figure 7.1b, the same site with the browser width 112
Figure 9.1	Using an ESP (Hubspot) to preview email display on various devices 126
Figure 9.2	Email AI ChatGPT suggesting five alternative subject lines 128
Figure 9.3	Using Google URL Builder to generate tracking code for an email campaign 131
Figure 9.4	Considering each step in the user journey and going beyond a 'last click' mentality 131
Figure 9.5	Litmus.com allows you to preview what your email will look like on a wide range of clients and devices 140
Figure 9.6	The easy-to-use interface for sending A/B split test campaigns using MailChimp.com 142
Figure 10.1	The 'single customer view' achieved by bringing all of our sources of information together 153
Figure 10.2	The challenges and reasons for CRM and ESP integration 156
Figure 10.3	Marketing automation is used in the nurturing and qualification stage of the sales and marketing process 158
Figure 12.1	Fake engagement on a Facebook page 180
Figure 13.1	Dashboard showing a 'primary' and 'indicators' 184
Figure 14.1	The custom report builder in GA4 192
Figure 14.2	This dashboard shows a 'primary' along with a number of 'indicators' as well as showing how the traffic sources have worked together (by using information from attribution modelling reports) 196
Figure 15.1	Extending the dashboard to include the contribution of offline experiences 200
Figure 15.2	Spreadsheet version of the digital branding dashboard 202
Figure 16.1	Working in the opposite direction to a dashboard and understanding the contribution of each channel 208

Tables

Table 3.1	Ideas for content-marketing themes	30
Table 3.2	Content-marketing themes and interactivity ideas	31
Table 3.3	User journey models and content mapping	33
Table 7.1	Discovery and engagement phases in mobile marketing	107
Table 13.1	Indicators and data sources for search traffic	183
Table 13.2	Indicators and data sources for social traffic	183

FOREWORD

The business environment is rapidly changing, and the fast-paced world of digital media is a constant challenge for organizations of all types. The meteoric rise of gen-AI over the past 12 months has only served to highlight this.

I passionately believe that marketing makes the difference to business performance. A key element of good marketing is understanding the power of branding. Branding is a tool that helps bring an organization's purpose to life, driving business growth, and enabling marketing to evolve and deliver on the triple bottom line, addressing not just profit but also people and the planet, leading to a shift in how we perceive our profession as a force for good. It's clear that knowledge of both the strategic impact and the tactical implementation of digital branding will become increasingly important.

Daniel has worked extensively with CIM, helping our members and customers navigate their way through this exciting and fast-moving environment. He is a respected authority on all things digital and, as such, is the ideal guide for your digital journey.

Chris Daly
Chief Executive
The Chartered Institute of Marketing

ACKNOWLEDGEMENTS

This is the fourth edition of this book, and it's been translated into more than a dozen languages. There are a lot of people this wouldn't have been possible without.

First, to the team at Target Internet. To Susana, Louise, Marie, Ciaran and Brad, I am extremely proud of what we have built together.

Thanks to everyone at the CIM for your ongoing support and partnership, with particular thanks to Chris Daly for his generous Foreword, and to James Sutton, James Delves and Bryndley Walker, for their ongoing support.

Many thanks to our generous and talented contributors: Gemma Butler, Tim Ruthven, Will McInnes, Bethan Jinkinson, Alistair Welham, Rachel Exton, Sarah Dawley, Jon Davids and Ciaran Rogers. I really appreciate your time and input.

A huge thank you must go to my publisher Kogan Page for their tolerance of the way I write (one big burst very close to the deadline!). To Jeylan Ramis and Donna Goddard for your patience and trust, and to Stephen Stratton for making this such a global success. And of course to Helen Kogan for leading such a great team and organization.

And, finally, a massive thank you to all of you who have read this book, visited Target Internet, listened to The Digital Marketing Podcast, followed me on social media and very kindly given me an audience to share my ideas and engage with.

Introduction

'Brand awareness' is an excuse used by marketers when they don't know the value of what they are doing. If they are asked the question 'how does that social media campaign impact the business?' and the answer is 'it's good for brand awareness', then it generally means they haven't got a clue. In a world of artificial intelligence (AI) generated content, deepfake audio and video, and huge levels of fake news, creating trusted brands has never been more important.

Most of us don't sell things online with a credit card payment facility. Most businesses have sales transactions in which the sale takes place somewhere other than our own website. It is therefore very hard to work out what the return on investment (ROI) is for the digital activity we carry out (particularly when we involve social media). 'Brand building' or 'brand awareness' are terms that are often used as the objective for work where the true objectives are not clear.

This book aims to demystify what brand actually is in a digital world, to show what it is doing for the bottom line, how it can be achieved and, most importantly, how it can be measured and improved.

This book will help you to build a robust framework for planning, implementing and measuring the effectiveness of your digital campaigns. This will mean that you are able to develop a measurable digital strategy based on clear objectives.

HOW TO GET THE MOST OUT OF THIS BOOK

The book is split into three key sections:

- **Part One: Digital branding in perspective**
  This part explores what we really mean by branding, and how this has completely changed because of digital marketing channels and technology. We also explore how fast-paced technology change in areas like AI is radically changing how we can build brands and trust in those brands. We explore what we really need to understand in order to be able to measure the effectiveness of our digital campaigns.

- **Part Two: The digital toolkit**

  This part looks at the practicalities of using all of the digital channels and tools available to us. We explore topics such as social media, mobile marketing and search optimization, while connecting them all up to the user journey of our target audiences.

- **Part Three: Digital brand strategy and measurement**

  In the final part we build a process for developing a digital strategy that can be implemented, measured and improved. We look at a robust framework for measuring all elements of our digital activity, including how to calculate the ROI of every activity we carry out. Most importantly it will be made clear how the strategies we develop are related to our business objectives.

To accompany this book there is an online resource of related materials, including podcasts, templates and tools. You can also get all the latest on digital branding by visiting **http://www.targetinternet.com/digitalbranding**.

PART ONE
Digital branding in perspective

Introduction

Let's start by saying what digital branding isn't. It isn't about logos or visual identity, and it certainly isn't about celebrity endorsements and big sports team sponsorships. What digital branding is really about is the sum of our online experiences. These online experiences may be influenced and impacted by logos and sponsorship, but we need to understand branding to be something much more than visual identity.

Branding has fundamentally changed because of digital media. Digital has led to two-way communications between brands and consumers – social media means that we can now talk directly with the brands that we use every day. In fact, most communications via digital media don't even involve the brand anymore and are now directly between consumers. We only need to look at review websites such as TripAdvisor to realize that what consumers are saying about us is more important than what we are saying about ourselves.

> **A TRADITIONAL VIEW OF BRANDING**
>
> When I say that branding isn't about visual identity or logos many people will be shocked. I'm not saying that these things are not important, but what I am saying is that they are an increasingly small part of a much more complicated

picture. Your logo and the visual aspects of your website design will certainly impact on a consumer's perceptions of your organization, and they mustn't be overlooked, but the reality is that we now experience things in our connected world in a much more complicated way than previously.

The number of different online touchpoints (points at which we are interacting with a topic, product or organization either directly via something such as a website or app, or indirectly via a search engine results page, an AI-powered chatbot or a social media discussion) we make before making a purchase are increasing. We are seeking more sources of information and are assigning trust differently. Gone are the days when marketing consisted of putting your product into the hand of a celebrity in a shiny 30-second TV commercial and thinking your efforts were complete.

This shift to dialogue rather than broadcast means that the traditional approach to branding is no longer sufficient. We need to understand how search, social media and mobile are impacting our target audience's perceptions of us and how it is impacting their likelihood of buying our products. We also need to do this in a measurable way.

It's all digital

Although this book is about digital branding, it is not only digital that creates your brand. It is every experience that your target audience has of you. From your call centre employees' tone of voice through to the type of paper you print your business cards on. The fundamental shift, however, is that all of these things are tied together by an online experience.

What do you do while you are watching TV? Well, according to GWI, 86 per cent of us will be second-screening on our mobile devices (GWI, 2024).

The reality is that our mobile devices are bridging the gap between our online and offline experiences, so that even broadcast media needs to carefully consider the online interaction it will cause.

Brand awareness as an excuse

I started this book by saying that brand awareness is a phrase that is often used as an excuse to justify digital activity that doesn't have clear objectives. Let's take an example. Many organizations have Instagram profiles. Yet most organizations have no idea as to why they have an Instagram profile. It's not to say that these Instagram business profiles are not valuable; they can be massively powerful. It's just that there is an awful lot of posting to social media for the sake of posting to social media.

There is a body of research called the Social Media Benchmark, a series of studies carried out by the Chartered Institute of Marketing looking at how organizations of all types are using and being impacted by social media. What is abundantly clear from each stage of this research, however, is that the majority of organizations are not using social media effectively, but they are doing more of it!

We will look at this in more detail in Part Two, Chapter 5. In this part we will explore what digital branding really is and how it means that branding has fundamentally changed.

BUSINESS TO BUSINESS

When we talk about brands and consumers it is easy to assume we are talking about a business to consumer (B2C) situation. In fact, all of the principles we are discussing equally apply in a business to business (B2B) environment as well. As the potential customer in a B2B scenario, we are still an individual going through a decision-making process. Although the buying cycle may be different and the decision-making process motivated by different factors, we can still map out and understand how digital branding is having an impact.

In reality, the process of mapping the impact and value of what we do online in B2B is even more apparent because the majority of B2B purchases are actually made offline and we need to understand what role digital is playing in making that sale.

What digital branding really means

01

A traditional view of branding says that a brand is: 'Name, term, design, symbol, or any other feature that identifies one seller's good or service as distinct from those of other sellers' (AMA, 2024). In fact, the word *brand* is derived from the Old Norse word *brandr*, meaning 'to burn', and was used in reference to marking cattle by burning the owner's brand onto them.

This idea of branding has been developed over the years to factor in a far more extensive set of considerations. As well as this idea of visual identity we may also consider the thoughts, feelings, perceptions, images, experiences, beliefs, attitudes and so on that are associated with a brand. This set of considerations builds up our *brand image*, and we may also talk about our experience of a brand as our *brand experience*. The best way of thinking about it, in my opinion, is that brand is the *personality* of something.

How digital has changed branding

If you could only get a feel for someone's personality by them telling you things about themselves, we may end up with a very shallow understanding of them. We may also have difficulty believing in the personality that has been constructed – and we may start to question the motivations behind what they are telling us about themselves. That is exactly the situation of commercial branding that uses broadcast channels such as TV. A personality is sculpted and then we are told what the personality is. We don't get to discuss, engage with and really understand the true personality.

Digital media now means, however, that the conversation is no longer one way. I can challenge, ask questions and develop a truer picture of the brand. I can see through a sculpted brand and start to see it for what it truly is. This can be a scary thing for many traditional brands. It can also be a huge opportunity.

> **BRAND DEMOCRACY**
>
> I was originally switched on to the idea of brand democracy by a good friend of mine and renowned inspirational speaker, Jonathan MacDonald. Brand democracy is the idea that your brand isn't what you say it is but rather the sum of what everyone else says it is. This has huge implications for not only how we manage our brands but also on how we need to change the very nature of our organizations.
>
> You can read Jonathan's original and often challenging thinking at **www.jonathanmacdonald.com**.

AI and branding

Artificial intelligence (AI) has had a profound impact on the world around us in very recent months and years. Things that were science fiction, or at least extremely difficult to do unless you had sufficient expertise and resources, are now made possible with tools available to everyone. These AI-based tools and their application can have a huge impact on our digital branding. This can be as simple as giving us the opportunity to create a better user experience by using machine learning to help us optimize a website experience (for example, by giving somebody content that is customized for them specifically) or by generating an image that follows our brand guidelines using generative AI.

However, beyond these AI tools that help us become more efficient and more effective, we also find ourselves faced with new risks and ethical challenges. Let's take a real-world example. Using a low-cost tool like Eleven Labs (https://elevenlabs.io/) I can create a completely convincing deepfake of my own voice. I can then type in any text I want and get the deepfake voice to read that text. The voice sounds exactly like me, and I can even generate the same speech multiple times, and each time it will sound slightly different and have ever so slightly different intonation, just as I would if I read the same thing multiple times. To test the quality of this voice, I replaced a segment of me speaking on the Digital Marketing Podcast, which has over 150,000 listeners. Nobody noticed. So if I can deepfake myself, do I need to even bother recording podcasts anymore? Do I need to inform my listeners? Legally I don't have to, but I would suggest ethically I should. If I trust you, and I suddenly find that after listening to your voice for some time, that it wasn't really you, it will damage my trust. AI gives our brands a huge amount of tools to improve what we do, but we also need to be careful how and when we use these tools, so we don't damage the trust in our brands. Any use of AI needs to done mindfully, considering the impact it may have. We'll explore the application of AI throughout this book, and consider how it can be useful, but also what risks it poses.

Global soapbox

If brand is essentially the personality of something, digital media gives us the ability and opportunity to understand the *true* personality of something. We can then use that understanding to help guide us in our decision-making processes.

This is a great opportunity from a customer point of view. For example, it means that instead of being put on hold for an hour when phoning a call centre and having little choice but to tolerate it, I can now go straight to one of many social media channels and make my frustrations very clear and very visible. I now have a global soapbox with access to all of the other potential customers out there, and I can impact a global organization's brand in a way that was not possible before (or, at least, was incredibly difficult). That highly visible complaint then becomes part of other people's brand perception (fairly or not) and suddenly the years of building a brand can be tumbled very quickly. This is a very much changed environment for businesses to operate in – if they ignore this change then it can lead to problems.

This ability to engage with and research into a brand can also be looked at from an even simpler point of view. Perhaps I am researching buying a car or a B2B service. I can now do a lot of research and inform my decision before I speak to the car dealership or service vendor. When I do make this final step I am far more informed and have developed a fairly in-depth perception of the brand before I engage directly with them. In fact, from information I glean online I may have opted out from even considering certain brands. That information may have been on a third-party website in the form of a review or comment from someone I have never met, but I may trust it over the voice of the brand itself.

> **BRAND PERCEPTION**
>
> If I search for you or your brand in Google or YouTube, what will I see? These search results, governed by the algorithms of these respective websites, represent what your potential customers will see when they search for you. Is it great branded content and satisfied customer reviews or bad news stories on third-party websites and negative reviews? Essentially you have control over what shows up, and a combination of creating great content, building advocacy, creating the right environment for gaining positive reviews and understanding and working with the platform algorithms is key to seeing the results that you want. With developments like the inclusion of AI-generated results in the search engines, it becomes even more essential for us to understand the complexities of where this information is coming from and how we can best influence every brand touchpoint our target audiences have.

Social media fail

This fast-changing environment and the slow pace of businesses to adapt to it is leading the social media disaster stories that we see on a daily basis online. Some of those stories will be highlighted later in the book in order to see what we can learn from them, but they generally have a number of things in common. Most social media disasters demonstrate a lack of knowledge of how to practically use a particular social media channel or show a belief that the brand can manipulate the channel in some way and get away from this need for authenticity and transparency. The other common theme is that of failing to understand the changed role of the brand in this two-way conversation. All of these themes will be explored in Part Two when we look at social media.

Traditional brand metrics

Traditionally, brand has been measured by asking questions and trying to judge what someone thinks of a brand, and trying to work out what this means in regard to potential sales.

There is a wide range of different ways of looking at this, but generally we would take some sort of sample survey of our audience and see what their attitudes were before and after exposure to some form of marketing. This survey would ask a range of questions, and there are lots of different approaches, but fundamentally we would look to answer the following questions:

- Are you aware of the brand?
- Do you like the brand?
- Do you intend to buy the brand?
- If you have purchased, do you intend to do it again?

Essentially, we are assuming that if we can get more people to answer positively to each of these questions, we are likely to get more sales. This can still be an extremely valid process, but only when effectively integrated into an overall approach, and we will explore this in more depth in Chapters 15 and 16.

Sum of all experiences

Essentially, digital branding is the personality of our organization, service or product created by the sum of all experiences that an individual has with that brand. This still includes things such as visual identity, but now also includes much more important and influential touchpoints such as social media interactions and online reviews. Your logo may make you recognizable, but it is your overall brand that decides what I remember you for.

Clarifying touchpoints

If we are defining digital branding as the sum of all experiences that an individual has with a brand, it seems straightforward to use the term 'touchpoint' to refer to one of these experiences (as we already have done). We do need to be careful, however, of the definition of a touchpoint. A touchpoint is often interpreted as some sort of engagement or experience with a marketing channel created by the brand. This idea of a marketing channel can be expanded to include everything from packaging to telephone calls.

Clarification is needed, though, when we go beyond these brand-controlled experiences to things like word of mouth and social media engagement. Very often these types of touchpoints will have no involvement with the brand at all, for example when a consumer reads an online review. Yet this is still a touchpoint and probably one of the most important of all touchpoints.

The role of digital transformation

Some of the changes we suggest in how you approach your digital branding simply require changes in how we use digital channels, but some go much deeper. You may need new systems and processes, or you may fundamentally need to drive culture change in your organization. This process of saying 'where are we now as an organization and where do we need to be to operate in this fast-changing environment?' is essentially at the heart of digital transformation. The environment in which our brands operate is moving very quickly, and will continue to do so. For this reason we need to create organisations that can adapt to change and not be disrupted by it. The aim of digital transformation is to create organisational agility to allow us to adapt to change effectively and quickly. Without the ability to adapt, our organizations cannot live up to our customers' expectations and this is why the principles of digital transformation are essential knowledge for anyone trying to build a brand. These key principles are great tools to assist you on your journey to improve your digital branding. As such I thought a few words from someone I respect and trust on the topic could give you some guidance when approaching any programme of great change.

VIEWPOINTS
Alistair Welham, Marketing Director

Alistair has over 25 years' experience in marketing and digital communications having specialized in financial services, real estate and car retailing. He teaches on the Imperial College Business School Digital Transformation programme, in addition to holding various senior marketing, trustee and consultative roles.

Tips for the digital transformer – views from my 'digital' chair

Sitting here in 2024 with the pandemic a distant memory and reconnected to the world, but differently, if anything digital transformation is accelerating. As an example, the explosion of AI tools and apps has brought excitement and fear in equal measure.

The digital change that was a necessity during the lockdowns has become par for the course, and on the less frequent occasions I venture out into the physical world, I realize just how much has changed.

I can travel from my home in the beautiful market town of Olney, around the globe and back again with all I need in a couple of devices. All monies, travel documents, presentations, backpack, and of course a passport. The immense power and complexity of this connected world goes unnoticed by many, but it has all been driven by the power of digital transformation.

It is further evidence that the statement by Karel Dörner and David Edelman from McKinsey (2015) 'digital should be seen less as a thing and more a way of doing things' continues to underpin how I think about digital transformation: we have to find new ways of doing things!

In my course 'Off on a Digital Journey', I talk about the art and science of digital transformation outlining five key steps for the digital marketeer looking to drive and implement change. These five steps still hold true in the post pandemic world and continue to be how I approach any large project or business change.

1. Defining the problem

It's such a simple starting point, but how many of us have found ourselves halfway through a project or programme only for someone to say, 'I'm not sure what we are building'? The time invested in clearly articulating who the target customer is, what their pain points are and how our solution is going to make the world a better place is fundamental to our ability to drive good digital change. I recommend you embrace the power of the 'value proposition canvas' in helping to shape an understanding of your customers and where to focus precious business resources, as this is a vital step for any group looking to transform.

2. Describe success

Wrapped up in the proposition discussion, the next crucial step is to define what 'good' looks like. Not just a clear articulation of the future state but the basis on which success will be measured. You will naturally create some specific financial measures and for the hard-nosed salespeople who expect a well-conceived sales funnel and plan. But often the most powerful measures are the softer ones and with increasing focus on the environment, sustainability and well-being, I'd encourage every business to include measures that focus on people and our planet.

3. Start small and plan to grow

Looking back, I would say most of my successes have grown out of small breakthroughs or initiatives; no one has ever rolled up to me with a multi-million-pound budget and said, 'go build me one of those'. But evidencing success through pilots, trials or concepts has captured the imaginations of even the toughest accountant and if you can demonstrate success, your gatekeepers will make the resources available. One of the more positive outcomes of the pandemic is availability and how easy it is to get a group of people together to kick around ideas and make plans. I am not deriding the value of a physical workshop or offsite, but a lot can be done in very little time using your preferred video channel and collaboration software.

4. Planning and measurement

The first role on my dream team is a competent planner, someone who can help shape our direction and co-ordinate the various people, agencies and functions to set out the plan. What is a plan without some great KPIs and how will we create these without access to the right data? It has been interesting to see how data has played such a vital part in the pandemic and the way people now naturally converse in percentages, ratios and forecasts as part of everyday language. If you can find a common language for your next project and a simple set of measures, you will be in a great place to set out a roadmap to your future transformation.

5. Create a movement

The past years have seen no shortage of movements, each with a powerful rallying cry that empowers the campaign, for example 'Black Lives Matter', or statements that capture the mood of a nation like the 'Cost of Living Crisis'. The power of words can be well used by anyone trying to effect change. Any movement starts with one person (makes me think of 'dancing guy' in the first follower YouTube clip), who brings together a small group of people who share a common vision or interest in making things better. The challenging part in organizations is getting enough of the right type of support, particularly given that often the most experienced digital natives are not those with the greatest authority or power. The good news is as human beings we are drawn to storytelling, and if you can find a way to create an attractive vision, a pathway to get there and a clear benefit for every stakeholder, you will be amazed how change can happen.

Take-outs

It is good to be 'back to normal' after the pandemic, although I'd say it's a different normal, and for my own part the benefits of improved hybrid working, focus on well-being, and the increasing desire to really make a difference in sustainability and climate change are real positives. This new world is the perfect environment for the 'digital transformer' who wants to make a difference and hopefully, in some small way, my thoughts and ideas can help you change your world.

Focusing on value

02

With all this talk of brand perception, social media engagement and changing business environments, it's easy to get distracted from the business and marketing fundamentals that are essential to our organization's success. This is especially true when the environment we are working in is changing so quickly, and it is easy to be distracted by what is new and 'shiny' rather than what is effective.

Fundamentally we need to be clear on two key things: first, we need to always have clear sight of what our business objectives are and to focus on how any marketing activity we are carrying out is connected to this. Second, we need to understand our target audiences' objectives so that we can align what they want with what we are offering. We need to understand their motivation. Everything else is really secondary to these two key points – and it is always good to get back to these fundamentals from time to time.

Bridging the gap

Traditionally, when we consider business objectives and target audience objectives, when these two things overlap we can see value. Value for both the business and the target audience (see Figure 2.1).

However, the reality of this in a digital environment is that this potential value is not enough. If I want you to engage with me online it is not enough for my product or service to just provide value. I have to give you a reason to want to engage, to leave feedback about my product or service, and to generally create dialogue.

This is where digital branding comes into play. Digital branding can bridge the gap between our business objectives and what my target audience actually wants to engage with (see Figure 2.2).

Figure 2.1   Aligned business and user objectives create value

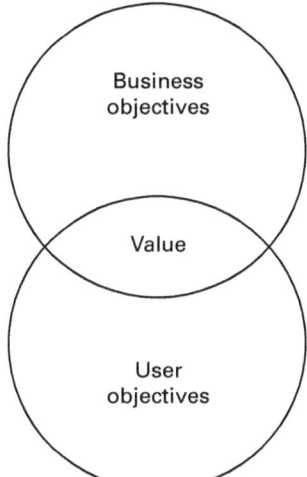

Figure 2.2   Digital branding bridges the gap between business objectives and target audience objectives

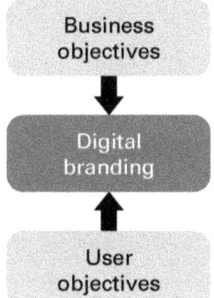

Value proposition

Value proposition is defined in a number of different ways by different people, but fundamentally it is a promise of value that should be appealing to our target audience – and that they believe will be delivered. It may be a promise of value in a single product or an entire organization. Your digital branding allows you to communicate this value proposition.

Let's take a look at a few examples from different markets to make things clear as to how all of this fits together.

Business to business service

If I want you to buy a complicated B2B service from me, I need to do a number of things, but most of all I need to give you the content you need to help you make a decision. This means I need to map out all of the stages of the buying cycle that you will go through and make sure that all of the different questions you need answered are covered. In most B2B situations the potential customer won't engage directly with a potential supplier until they have decided exactly what they want.

This may mean educating the audience on some topics even before they fully understand what I am offering. If this is an item that has a long buying cycle, or is a very occasional purchase, I will also need to engage with the audience when they are not actually in the process of buying yet. This means I must provide value beyond just talking about my solutions.

A standard digital branding approach here is for us to position ourselves as a useful resource on an industry topic and provide value through content. This could be anything from industry news, leadership articles through to in-depth reports, but the key thing is that I am providing value outside of just talking about what I do.

We need to measure the effectiveness of this content and what impact it is having in driving sales.

Consumer packaged goods

Many consumer packaged goods (CPG) are things like groceries and toiletries and are generally not highly differentiated. That is, many CPG aren't all that different from their competitor's products, so branding is very much what helps differentiate them. In fact, this is the market in which a traditional approach to branding was really developed. The problem in a digital world is why would I speak and engage online about detergent or confectionery?

This is where digital branding can bridge the gap between what a consumer wants to engage with and what an organization wants to talk about. By broadening the conversation and understanding our value proposition, we can find topics that a user will engage with. As examples: M&M's engage users with fun and quirky humour via Instagram – this creates repeat exposure and affinity with the brand; Dove use the theme of 'real beauty' to engage the audience and stimulate conversation – this creates exposure to the brand along with aligning the brand with positive topics. We need to measure the effectiveness of this social media engagement and understand what impact it is having in driving sales.

Complex consumer products

When we are buying a more complex consumer product, such as a car or a technology product, the process is actually very similar to the B2B process, even though that product may be purchased online.

A potential customer needs to understand the market and options available to them. We need to understand where they are in the buying cycle in order to provide the right content, and we may need to try to engage with them before they are even considering purchase, in order to build awareness and likelihood of purchase.

Charity funding

When a charity is seeking donations and potentially a long-term commitment to monthly donations, engagement is essential. It is essential so that I feel motivated to donate initially, but also so that I don't decide to stop donating and cancel my payment at some point.

Understanding motivations for donating becomes essential, and working out the value exchange that is going on can be very powerful. Social media allows for powerful personal connections, and by allowing individuals to portray themselves to their peers as they would like to be perceived, a charity can use their digital branding to provide great value for their audience, ie the charity can provide the mechanism via social media that makes the person donating look generous, caring or any other characteristic they would like to be associated with.

Luxury brands

With all this talk of value proposition and online touchpoints, you may be thinking of examples where this doesn't apply. The first and most obvious one is that of luxury brands. I have heard the argument many times that a luxury brand cannot be defined by a simple marketing process. Yet I would argue that exactly the same principles apply.

Your perception of a luxury brand is simply made up of all of the online and offline touchpoints that you have with that brand and its products. We have already said that digital branding is the set of digital touchpoints that shapes our opinions, and this is essentially no different.

Quite often, brands are developed over a number of years and this involves spending millions on advertising and placement in order to achieve the set of touchpoints to make you feel a certain way about that particular brand. You may see a celebrity using a product, see a brand in a certain high-profile event, or see a series of print ads that associate the brand with a luxurious lifestyle. These are simply touchpoints that are crafted to appeal to all sorts of human emotions and shape how you feel towards a brand.

It all comes down to content

All of the above examples show how we can use various digital channels to provide value, as long as we fully understand our target audience and their user journey. Digital branding is the sum of experiences that we have online and it relies on the provision of value. The provision of that value will generally rely on some form of content, which may be something that educates us around a topic and builds our trust, or content that we can share with our peers to make ourselves perceived in the way we would like to be perceived. Even when we are dealing with products that would generally generate little engagement, we can drive engagement through appropriate content and smart digital branding.

> Digital branding is the sum of experiences we have online and relies on the provision of value.

To do this well, however, we really need to focus on the user journey and see how we can provide value in order to influence the decision-making processes involved in purchasing anything. Understanding that user journey is exactly what we will look at in the following case study.

VIEWPOINTS
Tim Ruthven, External Engagement Director, UCL School of Management

Content is easy when brand and corporate strategy are one and the same thing

Impactful content is often elusive to HE marketers as they are rarely afforded the opportunity to collaborate with senior executives to define or calibrate the organization's value proposition. As a result marketers' brand- and product-level content marketing efforts are often at odds with customer needs as marketers work with ever-changeable value propositions that resonate poorly with an imagined consumer. Even worse, budgets are suboptimally allocated across tactical activity such as PR, PPC (pay per click) and social media, often amplifying vagaries that fail to build brand or generate leads.

When Imperial College London welcomed a new dean to lead its Business School, the dean immediately led a consultative process with the college and school community to define a target corporate brand identity and a strategy that would enable the school to compete on the global stage with the world's best.

This was the first successful attempt in the school's history to define itself and this provided the perfect opportunity for the marketing function to engage fully in the consultative process to ensure the school's vision, mission and strategic direction was one that would resonate with our key stakeholders, positioning the school with a distinct value proposition in the highly competitive global business school market.

Responsible for raising the profile of the school, I was acutely aware that with a supportive and decisive leader marketing could play a key role in defining the brand and potentially overcome the criticism we often faced as a function. Poor marketing was often seen as the cause for our low levels of brand awareness, undifferentiated messaging and fragmented visual elements when what was missing was a clear and distinct brand and organizational strategy.

I led the brand project for the dean, bringing in Max Du Bois, a recognized brand consultant, to help integrate what we needed in terms of brand within the dean's school level strategy. After two years of stakeholder engagement the school felt it had developed a vision, a mission, a suite of key messages for our audiences and a new visual brand that would help to position us distinctly over time among the best schools in the world.

I believe that without this foundation piece of work a content-led marketing approach would not have provided a satisfactory return on investment (ROI) for our organization. The strategy piece was challenging and time-consuming but ultimately provided us with the framework to communicate and build our brand in a distinctive and consistent way in what is a noisy marketplace. Our approach:

1   A bite-sized approach.
2   Upskilling the team.

3 Securing the support of leadership.
4 Aligning brand building with the strategic planning processes of our organization.
5 Seeking expert help.
6 Building content that provided 'points of proof' for our desired brand position.

1. A bite-sized approach

We broke the project into manageable parts that the organization could digest:

1 Measure brand awareness – this is irresistible insight that drives senior managers to act.
2 Align with leadership to define (or recalibrate) the brand – stakeholder expectations and current perceptions are also irresistible insight to senior managers.
3 Work with internal and external stakeholders to test and refine your messaging and target position – calibrate it to achieve the desired stakeholder response.
4 Start communicating the messaging – why wait for the pretty visuals to communicate to customers in a way that drives value?
5 Develop the visual brand to reflect the target brand position – it's time to look the part.
6 Continually scope for opportunities to build additional points of proof – when brand and organizational strategy are aligned, marketing is simply supporting and amplifying new initiatives.

2. Upskilling the team

We invested heavily in our people. We brought in digital consultant, educator and coach Daniel Rowles to work with us as a team to refine our brand strategy, identify our marketing skills gaps as individuals and as a team and guide us towards courses of study to build the necessary capability. We also recruited external experts to coach individual team members on projects over a six-month period to bed in the learning.

1 Bring in an expert to challenge your strategy.
2 Don't be afraid to discover the skill gaps in your team.
3 Fill your skill gaps.

4   Utilize coaching to ensure new skills and expertise impact current projects.

3. Securing the support of leadership

With the support of leadership we were able to run parallel projects to identify and engage with key stakeholders such as prospective students, research academics and the senior blue-chip executives. By understanding their needs, wants and desires we could better position the organization to meet them.

1   Secure the support of your leadership with irresistible insight.
2   Educate your senior executives with support from experts with distinguished track records.

Note: do not proceed until you have achieved this point. It may be necessary to wait for supportive leadership to arrive or to leave and find an organization with a leadership that has set a clear strategy.

4. Aligning brand building with the strategic planning processes of our organization

We realized that to enhance marketing ROI we had to support senior executives to develop the strategic direction. We presented insight that built a picture of how key customer stakeholders perceived the organization, what they needed, wanted and desired and how they felt our organization could deliver value they'd pay for. This insight dramatically impacted how the senior leadership wished to build and position the school. For example, it became obvious that the school lacked some academic disciplines that would be required to deliver distinctive research and teaching programmes needed by industry and society.

5. Seeking expert help

It is not often that a marketer gets to work with leadership to define a brand so bringing in experienced hands with such a critical project really paid dividends for us. Consultants must be experts in their field, match your organizational culture and have a strong track record of internalizing the expertise to manage the brand, eg willing to coach. Most importantly they must be willing to collaborate with other experts. We called on experts in brand strategy, visual brand, digital marketing, SEO (search engine optimization), PR and PPC. These were emerging fields where skill currency was, and still is, critical.

6. Building content that provided 'points of proof' for our desired brand position

With clear profiles of our target stakeholders and where we could reach them we worked to build a 'thought leadership' content hub to amplify the school's expertise. This conveniently translated in relevant keywords for PPC with excellent content reserved for amplification through PR and digital display brand campaigns. To achieve this integration we recognized the need to:

1. Partner with a PR agency who understood SEO and had the network to pitch our content.
2. Partner with a media agency capable of tracking and optimizing our PPC and display campaigns.
3. Develop a freelance team of journalistic professionals to write content aligned to our key messaging/words and attractive to media (the audience).
4. Partner with a videographer who understood social media.
5. Create an internal team capable of working with internal and external colleagues to plan, create, and curate brand-building content and schedules for its timely amplification.

By providing support to senior leadership, our marketing function was able to develop clear, distinctive and appealing communications, which resulted in a marked increase in the performance of our marketing and communications effort. The process was so successful that we feared a reduction in budget, but the performance of our marketing activity has actually achieved the opposite.

VIEWPOINTS

Bethan Jinkinson, Executive Editor, BBC Ideas

Why content and narrative are so important

I first got hooked on podcasts when someone recommended *Serial* series one to me. It blew my mind – it was a fascinating true-life tale, cleverly told and hugely addictive. After that, my podcast journey took me in all sorts of directions. From comedian Romesh Ranganathan's *Hip-hop Saved My Life* to the sublime *This American Life* (listen to the episode called 'Abdi and the Golden Ticket' – it's life-changing). My most recent addiction has been to Radio 4's *Sideways*, presented by Matthew Syed, which is brilliant at challenging preconceptions and giving me genuinely new perspectives on the world.

In my role as executive editor of BBC Ideas (short films for curious minds – bbc.com/ideas, check it out) I get a lot of inspiration from podcasts; they expose me to all sorts of ideas and corners of history. I always learn something from Malcolm Gladwell's *Revisionist History* (probably one of the best podcasters on the planet).

Podcasts have also exposed me to creative thinking in terms of my role as a leader. My favourite of that genre is Bruce Daisley's *Eat Sleep Work Repeat*, a fascinating podcast on workplace culture. Podcasts have also taught me more than I thought I wanted to know about economics (the BBC's *50 Things That Made the Modern Economy*) and food (the delightful *Table Manners* with Jessie Ware and her mum).

The best advice I can give an aspiring podcaster is to listen to tons by other people. What do you like about them? What grates on you? What made you click on one podcast and not another? Who has recommended podcasts to you, and what would you recommend? Develop your critical thinking and take inspiration from the ever-growing podcast world around you.

Something else to bear in mind is sound quality. I was a former digital editor at BBC World Service, the BBC's international radio network with a huge podcast footprint (including the seriously brilliant *Global News* podcast). Coming from a radio background you become really aware of the well-mixed, well-balanced and well-edited content. It really stands out.

Finally, remember that, for the listener, podcasting is an intimate medium. You make an active choice to listen. You can stop at any time, skip to another podcast. It's not like radio, which kind of washes over you and you're never quite sure what's coming next. So make every second count, keep the narrative driving forward, and keep surprising your listener. You want to give them insights and inspiration that they'll be talking about on social media, or down the pub. In my experience, word of mouth is a huge driver for discovery, so make sure your podcast is being talked about online and in real life.

Considering the user journey

03

So far we have discussed the idea of digital branding being the sum of all of your online experiences. We have also mentioned several times that managing this effectively requires understanding the user journey, so let's map this out in more detail and look at some of the tools that can help us along the way.

Multichannel marketing

The reality of all marketing is that it generally isn't just one thing that makes you buy a product or choose a supplier. Generally it is a huge range of factors that make you prefer one brand over another, choose a particular supplier or buy a particular product. Digital branding is all about understanding this process and making it measurable.

As marketers we can model, measure and use all sorts of tools to try to understand this buying process – and this is where digital marketing has its greatest strengths. We have access to more data and more ability to measure the user journey than ever before.

However, the missing piece in this measurement puzzle can be the interaction between online and offline marketing. Quite often mobile can act as the bridge between the two, yet we still face some challenges with this. The journey is very likely not to be a linear one: many channels and types of content may be revisited several times, and we may not have any visibility on some of the steps in the journey. However, we still have a better view than we have ever had before, and with a little planning we can fill in the gaps.

User journey examples

Let's take a look at two real-world user journeys – B2B and B2C – all the way through to purchase and consider how different channels are working together.

Business to business example

I need a new hosting company for my business website. I'm responsible for the website's reliability and I have had some bad experiences previously, ending in my website being offline, which left me feeling both frustrated and embarrassed. This buying decision is primarily motivated by risk mitigation, but I also need to make sure that my website will be fast and that any provider will give me the opportunity to expand and improve my web offering, so I need flexibility and performance. This is not a decision I will make without being well informed, and the user journey is made up of multiple steps, including but not limited to:

- doing numerous searches for suppliers;
- reading online reviews of these suppliers;
- signing up for newsletters from each of these suppliers;
- asking opinions on LinkedIn and Twitter from my social network of their experiences;
- completing several diagnostic tools to understand what kind of hosting I actually need;
- reading websites that talk about the technology behind hosting in order to educate myself about it;
- signing up for newsletters from the sites that helped me educate myself;
- talking to colleagues and trusted partners at unrelated events and meetings, getting recommendations for suppliers I had never heard of and making a note on my phone.

So let's map out what is important to note in this user journey. First, it is important that my decision is based on risk mitigation and finding the right fit to my needs. I also need to educate myself on the topic (which is very common in B2B buying decisions).

We also need to note the practicalities of this journey. It was done almost entirely online, except where face-to-face word of mouth was involved. However, I only knew that I should search for several of the suppliers because I was already aware of them due to some other offline interaction at previous trade shows. Also, much of the time I was reading and educating myself I was actually offline as I had no internet access (I was either on a plane or on a train with poor connectivity).

So what does this tell us about our digital branding? Well, our value proposition needs to align closely with the ideas of risk mitigation, trust and education. So a clear value proposition aligned to user needs at the heart of any strategy would be essential for any potential supplier. The suppliers need to provide more content than just telling me how great their solution is, and I need education in order to build trust. Together these elements convey a classic example of the need for content marketing, which we'll discuss shortly.

I had relied heavily on my social network and online reviews to influence my decision, so an effective social media approach was also clearly going to be essential for any potential supplier.

As well as needing these different types of content, I needed to be able to consume them in ways that suited me; and what suited me varied by time and place. I need content that will work on all of my devices.

Business to consumer example

I'm looking at what I can do with my airline loyalty points, how the process works and where I might like to go. This process is as much about enjoying the process of looking at the destinations I could visit as it is about making any sort of practical plan.

As I work through this process I will make a number of steps that may include but are not limited to:

- trying to log into my account online to see how many points I have;
- understanding the process of using the points to book flights;
- seeing how far the flights can take me – and obtaining a list of available destinations without having a particular destination in mind;
- understanding when flights are available;
- looking at the destinations, exploring holiday options and looking at the suitability for different types of travel (romantic, family, etc);
- working out the most cost-effective way of using my points, considering airport taxes and other charges.

Bear in mind that I said this was as much about fun as it was about practical planning. I cite this example because not only is it real, but with my particular airline of choice it turned out to be nearly impossible. The key point here is that it was essential to understand the motivation of my user journey, and that was to explore, to learn and to 'mock plan'. Let's take a look at some of the issues that got in the way of this process meeting my requirements:

- main website redirecting to mobile website with limited functionality;
- no ability to go back to main website easily;

- main website not designed to work on multiple devices;
- search options not suited to my user journey of being unsure of my final destination;
- no easy way to browse availability without browsing through page after page of dates;
- no further information or recommended sites on potential destinations;
- unclear guidance on travel options when travelling with family (I will not be popular if I'm sitting in business class sipping cocktails and waving to my family who are seated in economy).

These are not just technology issues. After all, the airline had an app. They just hadn't thought through the different user journeys, and the process had been mapped to work with their booking system.

If these journeys were embraced, any airline or holiday company I was looking up would have the opportunity to engage me, reinforce their brand and give me inspiration for future travel. Even if it didn't lead to me booking there and then, by making the process easier they could improve my brand loyalty and potential word-of-mouth recommendations.

This point of it not leading to an immediate booking is an important one and is at the heart of mobile branding. I may go through the whole flight-booking process only to drop out at the final step. This may not be because something went wrong, but rather that I was using the tools available in order to *plan* rather than make a booking. I may then go through the same process a month later and actually make a booking. I need to be able to understand this journey and attribute value to the original visit that didn't end in a sale. This is something we'll explore more and, in fact, we can solve this initially complicated-looking scenario simply by using some free web analytics software (such as Google Analytics and Microsoft Clarity, which we'll explore later).

Content marketing

Content marketing is often talked about when looking at user experience and search optimization (two things we'll look at in Part Two), but it is also very much part of your approach to digital branding. Fundamentally, content marketing is about providing useful and engaging content that is suited to the user's journey. Generally, content marketing is about providing value beyond your direct product offering. If we go back to my example of selecting a hosting provider, a useful focus for content marketing would have been educating the user about web technologies. A few more examples are set out in Table 3.1.

Content marketing, value proposition and brand

Content marketing allows us to bolster our value proposition through digital-delivered content or services. More importantly, we have the opportunity to use digital technologies creatively to deliver this value proposition via interaction.

Table 3.2 takes our ideas for content-marketing themes and looks at how they could be applied in an interactive way.

All of these very simple ideas could be developed into something far more robust that would interactively reinforce a brand value proposition. It is important to understand how this can be applied to organizations with completely different products or service offerings. A B2B service is generally a high-involvement purchase. That is, you think carefully and do some research before buying. Buying confectionery, on the other hand, is generally a very low-involvement purchase – you're unlikely to go online and compare chocolate bars before buying them! However, using digital-delivered services and content marketing can help bolster value proposition and brand positioning in both cases.

Table 3.1 Ideas for content-marketing themes

Type of company	Focus of content marketing
SEO agency	Digital marketing advice
White-water rafting (aimed at teams)	Team building and human resources
Alcoholic drink brand	Cocktail-making and recipes
Detergent	Family money-saving tips
Sportswear	Training and fitness tips
Business service	Thought leadership articles

Table 3.2 Content-marketing themes and interactivity ideas

Focus of content marketing	Interactive idea
Digital marketing advice	Campaign reporting tool
Human resources	Interactive HR guide with scenario planning
Cocktail-making and recipes	Interactive portable recipe book
Family money-saving tips	Coupons and location-based savings
Training tips	Training-objective progress tracker
Thought leadership articles	Interactive audio/video tutorials

The stages of the user journey

Any online journey goes through a number of different stages, starting with a lack of awareness about a topic all the way though to direct commercial intent and post-purchase loyalty (or lack of!). There is a wide range of different models that can help us visualize this, but I think considering a traditional sales funnel is a great place to start.

Traditional sales funnel

A traditional sales funnel (Figure 3.1) sees our target audience move from no commercial intent and general browsing or having a vague notion on a topic, through to having an active interest, on to the actual point of purchase and finally into the potential loyalty stage.

What the diagram also shows is that this journey is not necessarily a linear one. I may spend an extended period of time browsing and revisiting content before I ever move on to the active interest phase. Also, the duration of the active interest phase will vary according to product/service offering and target audience. Once into the loyalty stage I may also find content intended for the browsing stage useful again.

With each stage of the journey I need to understand my target audience's objectives and motivations and work out what content and interactions will drive them to the next stage. We'll look at how we can map content against this funnel in a moment.

Figure 3.1 The sales funnel

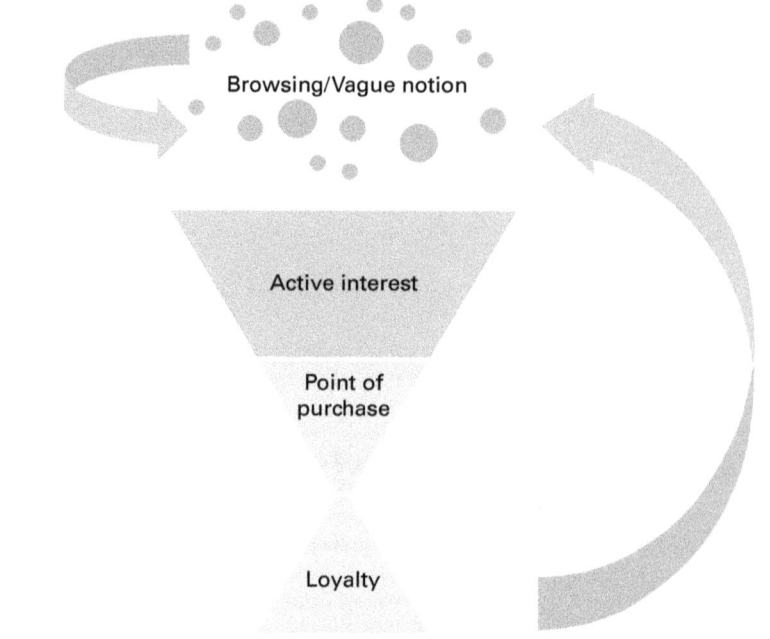

Figure 3.2 Avinash Kaushik's See, Think, Do, Care framework

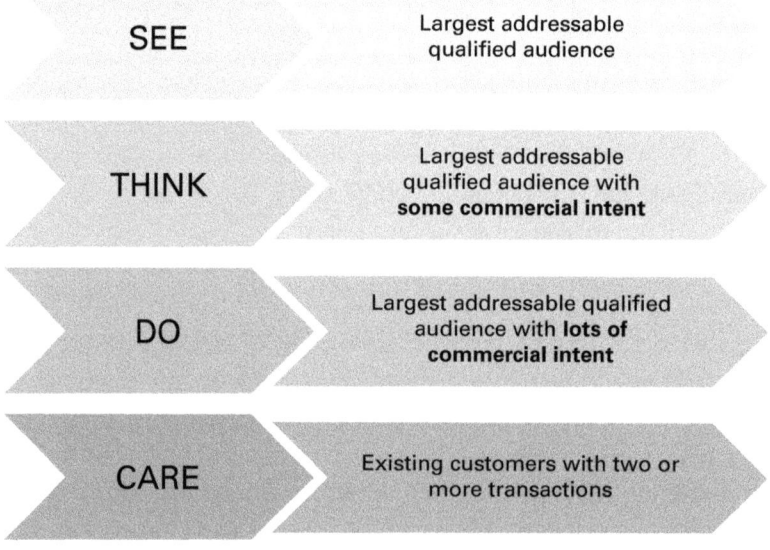

See, Think, Do, Care

Avinash Kaushik is a best-selling author, renowned analytics expert and a digital marketing evangelist for Google. Through his excellent blog, Occam's Razor, he has described his very useful See, Think, Do, Care framework (Figure 3.2). You can read more about it at **http://www.kaushik.net/avinash/**, but it is a simple to understand yet very flexible and effective model for planning content.

In reality, our funnel model and the See, Think, Do, Care framework are actually telling us the same thing. We need different content in different contexts for each stage of the user journey.

Content mapping

So let's take a couple of examples and look at how we can map content against each of the stages of both user journey models. We'll take two very different organizations: **TargetInternet.com**, a business to business organization that sells access to online digital marketing courses, and **Tesco.com**, a global online grocery retailer. Table 3.3 shows the four stages of the user journey (from both user journey models) and then shows examples of content at each stage for a particular audience.

The see/browse content is of broad general interest to our target audience. The think/active interest content is actively related to what the organizations sell. The do/point of purchase is their key product offering. You'll notice the content at the see/browse stage can also be used at the care/loyalty stage.

Table 3.3 User journey models and content mapping

Stage	TargetInternet.com	Tesco.com
See(Browse)	7 top Instagram tips for social success	25 things to do with your children on a rainy day
Think(Active Interest)	Complete guide to bridging the digital marketing skills gap	20 healthy ideas for children's lunch boxes
Do(Point of Purchase)	Online digital marketing courses	Online grocery shopping
Care (Loyalty)	7 top Instagram tips for social success	25 things to do with your children on a rainy day

Value proposition and user journey

Once we map out and understand our different target audiences, their different motivations and the user journeys they could potentially take, we start to have the basis of a digital plan. Once we align this to our business objectives and can measure for success and improvement, we have the makings of a digital strategy.

The third and final section of this book will give you a measurement framework to bring all of these things together.

Mapping the user journey

Now we can start to understand how we can consider each step of the user journey. What we also need to start thinking about is how we can use the different digital channels appropriately in order to achieve our goals.

In Part Two we will look at the practicalities of each of the digital channels, and in Part Three we will build a step-by-step process for developing our digital branding and looking at how we can measure it. However, before we get there let's take a quick look at the practicalities of each stage of the user journey and how different channels can be used effectively.

Let's consider an example, and think about the role of social media in the user journey. If we take any user journey model, such as Google's See, Think, Do, Care or the Attention, Interest, Desire, Action framework, we can factor in social media at any of these stages. However, how we apply social media at each of these stages should be different. Let's work through each of the stages of the See, Think, Do, Care model and consider how social media fits in.

At the See stage, we are just doing what we do every day and have no particular interest in a particular product or service. I am likely to browse through social media for personal or general business interest, listening to my favourite podcasts and watching video channels that I regularly watch. The opportunity here is to provide me with something useful or entertaining that may get my attention or drive a visit to a social media post, web page or other content.

At the Think stage, I have taken an interest in the topic area but not necessarily been actively interested in your product or service. Here I could share content that grows your interest and develops a relationship between the potential customer and my brand.

At the Do stage, you actively want what I am offering and I can use targeted social media to try to drive an action. I should only do this if I am already aware that you are interested in my product/service or other offering so I don't bombard other people with irrelevant sales messages.

At the Care stage, I have already transacted with you, and I have the opportunity to build loyalty, encourage you to post feedback (which in turn may be relevant in somebody else's journey at the Think and Do stages) and to continue building a relationship to encourage repeat custom and/or advocacy.

We can see from these different stages that if I try to put the wrong content in front of you at the wrong time, it will be irrelevant at best and could quite possibly be irritating and damage my brand.

GOALS AND CONVERSIONS

At this stage, it is worth defining some terminology that will be important throughout this book: a *goal* is something we want our target audience to do, generally on our website. This could be buying something, but it could also be the filling in of a form, downloading something or just visiting a particular page; a *conversion* is the completion of a goal.

By tying these activities back to our social media and other digital channel activity, we can start to understand how they are contributing towards our online objectives.

BUILDING A BRAND THAT CONNECTS WITH CUSTOMERS, JON DAVIDS, CEO INFLUICITY

The following is a modified excerpt from Marketing Superpowers, *published 18 June 2024 by Jon Davids.*

Every marketing class talks about the importance of building a brand. And while there's a lot of precedent to it, I think the idea of a brand is daunting. Especially to a small business.

I also think the polished brand giants of today were mostly built in the boardroom. And that won't work anymore.

So let's talk about a new idea.

Instead of trying to create a brand, you should create a movement.

When I say movement, I'm actually trying to move people from one place to another. Ideally, towards your belief. It's the one thing you're trying to push. It's the core of your brand promise.

That movement doesn't need to be lofty or even serious. It just needs to relate to your area of expertise and your brand.

- If you make fruity bubble gum, your movement could be about how amazing fruity bubble gum is. Much better than mint.
- If you sell smart irrigation systems, your movement is about how people need to stop wasting water and upgrade their lawn care technology.
- If you're a real estate agent in Boston, your movement is about how fantastic it is to live in Boston. After all, you want people to move there. (Literally.)

As you can see, these don't need to be serious or heavy topics. Not curing diseases, stopping wars or eliminating crime. We're doing simple things. You are creating a core belief in something and getting others to believe it with you.

But I know that creating a movement can still seem lofty. It's difficult to know where to start. That's why I created a formula to make it simple. I call it the Movement Formula.

The Movement Formula

There are three factors behind every movement (Figure 3.3).

1 A *unifying belief* that enhances [good thing] or reduces [bad thing]
2 *Faith* that this is the best way to do it
3 *Actions* towards achieving that thing

When you have those three ingredients, you have a movement.

Let's look at this formula another way:

You start with a unifying belief that people can get behind and multiply it by giving people faith in that unifying belief. The strength of that belief and the faith behind it equals the action those people take. And by 'action' I mean sales. After all, they'll take action in your movement by buying the thing you're selling.

The reason that the unifying belief is *multiplied* by faith is simple: If there's zero faith, the belief is worthless. If there's a little bit of faith, the belief will be minimal. If you can multiply faith by 10, or 100 or 1,000, the belief will be off the charts. More importantly, the action will follow in exact

Figure 3.3   The Movement Formula

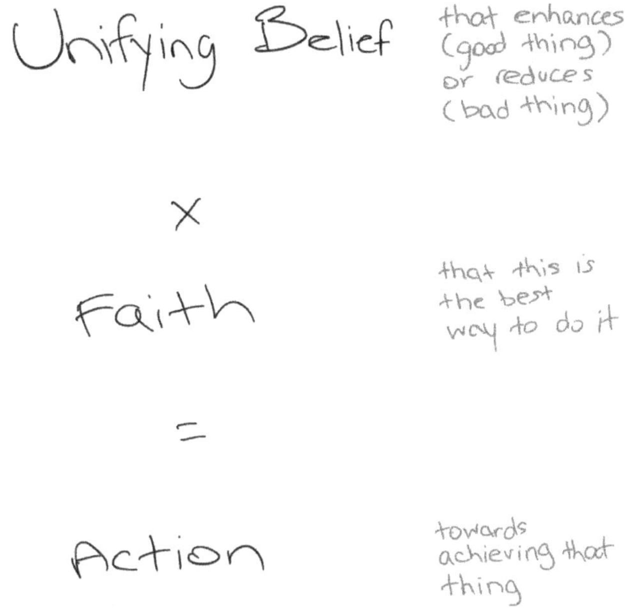

Unifying Belief — that enhances (good thing) or reduces (bad thing)

×

Faith — that this is the best way to do it

=

Action — towards achieving that thing

proportion. That's what happens with world-class movements. They can literally alter culture and society.

This is very simple math. And I'm really not good at math. So if I get this, you certainly can too.

Let's look at each ingredient more closely.

1. A unifying belief that enhances [good thing] or reduces [bad thing]

Being an influencer is about getting others to believe the thing you tell them. Within that they need to know you, like you, and trust you. And to win them over you'll need to offer something that gives them more of what they want (ie a good thing) or eliminates something they hate (ie a bad thing).

If I'm a travel agent who helps people plan exotic vacations, and you're someone who loves exotic vacations, then my unifying belief helps you enhance your 'good thing' – taking exotic vacations.

If I'm a cyber security expert who helps people avoid data breaches, and you're someone who wants to avoid data breaches, then my unifying belief helps you reduce your 'bad thing' – a data breach.

If I'm a math tutor who teaches you how to solve difficult math equations, then my unifying belief helps you increase your 'good thing' – being good at math.

These are all clear examples of enhancing a good thing or reducing a bad thing. That is effectively what a movement is all about.

And notice that the unifying belief is something that your target audience wants. That doesn't mean *everyone* wants it. Some people may not be interested in exotic vacations, or data breaches, or being good at math. In fact, some people might be against those things. For all sorts of reasons.

Movements rarely have universally held beliefs. Rather, they unite under a set of beliefs that one group of passionate people can get behind. But not everyone.

Think about cultural touch points like sports, music and politics. One thing that drives fans to be passionate about their 'team' is that there are so many detractors. People who are against the movement. They might also have an opposing movement.

The key is to appeal to the people that you want to target. Who is your target customer? Don't worry about all the people who don't share your belief. With any luck, they'll become vocal haters and drive more growth for you, by rallying the believers.

I'll talk about the importance of haters in Section 8. But for now, just understand, haters are a good thing for your movement.

This is absolutely not supposed to be a 'universal' belief. It is a 'unifying belief'. There's a big difference.

2. Faith that this is the best way to do it

Once you've established the unifying belief, you must instil faith that this is the way. Faith can be challenging because it's illogical.

Faith is belief without hard evidence. In the case of a travel agent who plans exotic vacations, there's no proof that this particular travel agent is the best in the world. After all, what does 'best' even mean? And if there were an agreed upon definition, how would we evaluate that? I obviously can't speak to every travel agent in the world.

This goes back to the main character at the core. If they've done an effective job building KLT, then the brand has a good shot at instilling faith.

There are also varying degrees of faith. Some people are devout without question. Some are constantly questioning. And their faith deepens or weakens over time. You need to always be pushing faith forward. It's the glue that holds your movement together.

3. Actions towards achieving that unifying belief

Once you have a unifying belief that multiplies with faith, the last step is action. What action can your believers take to achieve that outcome?

Let's go back to my examples from before.

If I'm the travel agent pushing exotic vacations, believers can take action by going to those locations. Tasting the food. Drinking the wine. Breathing the air.

If I'm the cybersecurity expert pushing data protection, people can take action by using strong passwords, software updates, running backups and using multi-factor authentication.

If I'm the tutor pushing math education, people can take action by taking courses, practising the equations, collaborative learning, writing tests, and applying math to their work.

But remember, each of these people is selling their solution. Travel, cyber security, math education. That's the product. That's the revenue. That's why the movement exists. Once you create the unifying belief and multiply it with faith, the only logical step is to sell the solution.

We need to give people something to do. And make it accessible for them to take action. After all, if I'm the main character with a movement behind me, I want people to move. To go from point A to point B. And of course, as a marketer, I want this movement to drive sales.

Those three ingredients make up the Movement Formula.

Unifying Belief × Faith = Action

Now let's look at some powerful movements and see how they use the Movement Formula.

Chapter 12: Movements all around us

Lasting movements are all around us. Some of these have been around for years, decades or centuries. To be clear, these are not single company movements. I'm using these as examples to show you how effective and timeless they are.

Example #1: The ketogenic diet

1. Unifying belief that enhances [good thing] or reduces [bad thing]

Consume less carbs, eat more fat and protein and you'll lose weight.

2. Faith that this is the best way to do it

- Celebrities and athletes who follow the Keto diet like Halle Berry, Kim Kardashian, Lebron James, Tim Tebow and others.
- Health and medical influencers who talk about Keto like Dr Josh Axe and Dr Eric Berg.
- Food companies who develop Keto friendly foods making it easier for people to adopt this style of eating.

3. Actions towards achieving that unifying belief
- Eat lots of meat, eggs, and vegetables.
- Avoid grains, sugars, and processed foods.
- Limit your carbohydrate intake.
- Follow a meal plan.

According to UC Davis, the global addressable market for the Keto Diet is $11–12 billion in 2022. That's a whole lot of avocado-oil mayonnaise, high-fibre tortillas, and protein cookies. If you're a believer in the keto diet, you'll take action by purchasing these products.

Notice how the keto diet combines a powerful unifying belief with faith-building validation. There's plenty of action people can take to follow the movement, including buying lots of stuff tailor-made for them. Nothing helps you express belief quite like a dollar.

This is a clear example of a movement in action.

Let's look at another one.

Example #2: Value investing

1. Unifying belief that enhances [good thing] or reduces [bad thing]

Buy stocks that are trading for less than their intrinsic value and make more money.

2. Faith that this is the best way to do it
- famous value investors like Benjamin Graham and Warren Buffett;
- dedicated investment funds and vehicles;
- decades of evidence for its success;
- books and courses on this topic;
- social media discussion and debate around the topic.

3. Actions towards achieving that unifying belief
- evaluating stocks based on value investing principles;
- reading financial reports;
- investing with a margin of safety;
- putting your money in value investing funds.

Value investing touches on something that most people want. To make more money and lose less money. It uses that motivation to create a simple unifying belief.

Anyone who is moved by this unifying belief can read countless books and articles on the topic. This will strengthen their belief and faith in the value investing approach.

As for action, there's a lot of it. You can certainly invest your own money and follow the guidelines of value investing. Or you can entrust your cash with an investment fund whose focus is on value investing. These come in all flavours, with names like small-cap value funds, dividend value funds, quantitative value funds and so on.

You can be sure there are plenty of money managers who are getting paid to handle your money. All thanks to the movement of value investing.

And now let's look at the mother of all movements. Get ready – this is a big one.

Example #3: Organized religion

1. Unifying belief that enhances [good thing] or reduces [bad thing]

Follow the teachings of God and you'll go to heaven.

2. Faith that this is the best way to do it

- prominent religious leaders throughout society;
- compelling stories, characters, and lessons;
- visibility in media and entertainment;
- schools and educational programs;
- family traditions and rituals.

3. Actions towards achieving that unifying belief

- go to church, temple, etc;
- give to charity;
- don't steal;
- be kind to your neighbours.

Religion is my favourite example of a movement. Because it was likely the earliest and most enduring movement in human existence. I'm not referring to any one religion specifically, but religion more broadly. And because it is taught in society from such an early age, it resonates with people more strongly than almost any other movement.

The unifying belief is simple and clear. Humans have a great desire to find purpose in their life. Wondering about the meaning of it all. What happens before we're born or after we die? What is the difference between good and evil? How can we serve a higher purpose?

Religion has it all.

Faith is instilled in people early and often. And there is plenty of action to take if you are a religious person.

As an example, let's look at the Catholic Church. I'm using this only because there's a good amount of public information on the money involved in the Catholic Church. And we're talking about lots of money.

It's hard to quantify exactly how much money the Catholic Church generates. The tithe alone is worth a ton. That's where every member of a church donates 10 per cent of their income to the church. But it gets much bigger than that.

A report by Yale Climate Connections in 2021 reveals that the Catholic Church owns 177 million acres of land across the globe for its churches and schools, along with farmland and forest land.

There's big money in this movement. And it's been around for a couple thousand years. That's serious staying power.

And it goes even further. The most iconic movements encourage people to take action together. Sports teams have stadiums. Politicians have rallies. And religions have temples. Bringing people together amplifies the unifying belief and the faith. That all leads to more action.

Objectives and authenticity

04

It sounds obvious, but every piece of marketing activity that will help to build your digital branding needs to have a clear connection to your business objectives. If we are to build a LinkedIn page, tweet five times per day or build an iPhone app, we need to be very clear about how it is contributing towards our bottom line.

I know, for example, that by posting to LinkedIn a number of times per week I will drive traffic to my website, because I link back to the content I produce. I will also build my LinkedIn following, because my content gets shared, and so I will have a larger audience to share with in future. This social activity will help to persuade the search engines that my website has authority by giving it the 'social signals' it needs to move me up the search rankings. This in turn will lead to more visitors to my website because of increased search visibility. The engagement with my content drives trust and improves the perception of my site.

These may seem like great things to aim for, and they are, but in reality I'm only doing them because a certain percentage of traffic and audience can then become paying customers. Without focusing on this sharp end of the sales funnel, I am producing volume for the sake of it. After all, I can have a million LinkedIn followers, but it doesn't necessarily mean that I'll ever sell anything.

We can spend a huge amount of time, effort and resources on digital branding, which if not properly aligned to our business objectives will not produce results. In light of this risk, this chapter is dedicated to exploring a case study of one of my favourite digital branding campaigns that ultimately failed. Something that on initial inspection seemed like a stroke of genius in digital branding, but that ultimately failed to achieve business results and was unceremoniously dumped and replaced with a very traditional approach to branding. The brand in question even produced a case study that talked about how putting your product into the hands of a celebrity was no longer a suitable approach to branding – and now they had taken a new approach, one that may on superficial inspection seem to reflect the ethos of what we are trying to promote in this book. Essentially, though, the approach used did not drive sales, and we need to understand why this was the case.

Branding for differentiation

The brand in question was Pepsi and the campaign I'm referring to was the Pepsi Refresh Project. If you are based in the United States it is fairly likely that you're aware of the project, but outside of the United States it didn't really get much coverage. When I heard about it, and watched the case study video, I fell in love. I suddenly thought that a massive brand had really got it – and I was convinced initially that it would be a success. You already know that it wasn't, but let's talk through the mechanics of what they did and look at what, on first inspection, looks like excellent digital branding (and, in fact, much of it is absolutely excellent).

Pepsi already knew that trying to differentiate on product alone was futile. Even their own video case study states very clearly that even though Pepsi and Coca-Cola taste slightly different, they are both 'brown, fizzy, soda pop'. I should mention at this time that the original description in the video was 'brown, fizzy, sugar water' – that version of the video disappeared pretty quickly!

This was a fairly bold way of approaching things. They then went on to say that you *could* put your product in the hands of a superstar in a 30-second shiny Super Bowl commercial (the most expensive TV advertising slot in the world) but that they were going to do something different.

By the time I got this far I was very excited. To tell your customers something they clearly already knew, but that had never really been admitted, was honest and exciting. Pepsi made it clear that their product was very similar to other products on the market and that they had been marketing by using celebrity mega productions. Wow, I was impressed.

Then they blew my mind. They said that the Pepsi Refresh Project would give away the US $20 million they were going to spend on their Super Bowl commercials to good causes. And that the audience could select the good causes by voting via social media. I was massively impressed, and so were a lot of other people. It gained huge coverage. It was a news story in its own right. Millions of people voted. I used it as a case study at every presentation and keynote that I did for months, and I still use it to this day.

So, with this great idea, what happened next? They ended up closing it down (quietly) and moving back to a strategy of aligning with celebrities. Why? Because it didn't generate sales. We really need to understand why.

Authenticity

I think we can sum up in a few words why the Pepsi campaign didn't work. It wasn't authentic. Now, I don't mean that they weren't donating all that cash, and I certainly don't mean that they lied in any way. What I mean is that this digital branding wasn't truly authentic with who they were.

There are a couple of telltale signs that really make this stand out. It was a project; we describe it as a campaign – both of these things generally imply that it has a beginning and an end. For this truly to have changed things, it needed to be the start of an ongoing commitment to a value proposition around making the world a better place. The thing is, we all knew that even though this was a great project, Pepsi wasn't suddenly some sort of social enterprise or charitable foundation (they actually do have a charitable foundation and you can find what good work they do in the call-out box below). We knew this was a marketing campaign to make us buy more fizzy drinks. This tells us something fundamental about how digital branding has to be different from our traditional ideas of branding. A brand can't just tell us that it represents something and then assume we will believe it. The brand needs to live its values and then has the opportunity to communicate this via digital branding.

> **LET'S BE FAIR**
>
> I want to make it clear at this stage that I really respect Pepsi for being bold enough to try the Refresh Project in the first place. I also respect their decision to can it (pun intended) when it didn't work. Since then (and before) they have embraced a huge range of great digital initiatives.
>
> As for that charitable foundation I mentioned, you can find it at the link given below, but for example the foundation gave over $47 million to good causes in 2023 alone, more than double the $20 million mentioned in the Pepsi Refresh campaign.
>
> The PepsiCo Foundation: https://www.pepsico.com/our-impact/philanthropy/pepsico-foundation.

Authentic value proposition

I have stated that your digital branding is there to deliver your value proposition. What we also need to be clear on is that your value proposition has to be completely authentic. If you say that you are committed to making the world a better place, you really should live by those words. If your digital branding says that you truly care about customer service, you really should care. Everyone in your organization needs to feel personally responsible to deliver this value proposition. That is because it is a promise, and none of us like to have promises broken.

There is nothing all that new in this idea, but digital branding means that we cannot hide behind hollow promises any more. For example, consider how the public reacts when a politician who is campaigning for family values has an extra-marital affair (a timeless example) – it feels even worse when we are let down by the very person who said they understood what we wanted and shared our values.

The digital world we live in means that there are many more ways for our lack of authenticity to be exposed. This transparency means that we can build powerful brands based on real promises faster than ever before. That same transparency means that a lack of authenticity will be exposed.

VIEWPOINTS

Gemma Butler, Sustainable Marketing Consultant, Co-Founder – Can Marketing Save the Planet Ltd, and author

Since I first shared my viewpoints back in 2020 on the need for marketing to step up and face the growing environmental crisis and the need for 'sustainable transformation', the operating landscape has changed somewhat. Increased regulations and guidelines on green claims, the rise of greenwashing and greenhushing, increasing external pressures continuing to mount from consumers, employees and investors, and measures taken to make sustainability reporting a mandatory requirement as the urgent need for transparency continues have all happened.

The need for business and indeed marketing to step up and play a significant role in raising awareness, educating and shaping behaviours when it comes to the environmental and societal challenges we face remains evident. Marketing needs to look at the role it has played and the role it can play in delivering a better future, sustainable markets and new opportunities. Sustainability continues to be the biggest challenge we face today as well as being one half of the biggest conversations happening in business, the other half of the conversation is artificial intelligence (AI) and, at this stage there is only one certainty, both will change how business operates in the future. Growing external pressures and demand from people for more transparency means brands and businesses need to communicate their responsible and sustainable practices and stand up for the things they are passionate about, stepping beyond the pledges and commitments and taking action.

The changing operating landscape gives marketers a huge opportunity to be part of the solution and bring their key stakeholders on the journey with them. Sustainable marketing isn't about totally reinventing marketing but rather about rethinking all guises of marketing through a responsible lens. Marketers need to continue to champion getting back to the 'core of the brand' – communicating and aligning organizational purpose, values and brand across the entire value chain of a business. Keeping pace with innovation, insights, sentiment, data and opinion is vital.

The need for marketing to grow its own awareness and understanding of what is happening in the macro environment has only grown stronger. Marketers need to be aware of the regulations on making green claims, connecting the dots, removing the jargon and ensuring terms such as net zero and circularity are understood and relevant for people so they can take action. And, they need to keep the conversations going, communicating with confidence, internally and externally.

How marketing communicates what needs to be done considering how they can align and support sustainability and wider organizational agendas is a priority every chief marketing officer should be thinking about. The narrative and storytelling to be able to meet your audiences where they're at and the use of words and language which go beyond the transactional relationship of just selling products is key to long-term relationships and customer and employee loyalty, which drives ongoing positive impact for both the organization and society.

In a world that continues to change at pace one thing remains and that is marketing's remit is far more diverse than business realizes, going beyond just advertising and selling 'stuff'. The diversification of skills required in the marketing function remains broad; skill building for the sustainability transition should be a top priority of any business alongside digital. The need to equip marketers so they can operate in their current roles and be ready for future roles is imperative. Sustainability isn't just about the environment, it's about the sustainability of the organization itself and the value it creates for those who engage with it.

Marketing can and must be a force for good!

Authenticity, AI and deepfakes

All this talk of authenticity and living up to our promises has now entered a new era of potential distrust. With the arrival of AI deepfakes, in audio, image and video format, we are all increasingly distrusting of what we see and hear. Even before these deepfakes, fake news has had a huge impact in people's trust of what they read, see and watch. Social media algorithms have further fuelled the problem by creating echo chambers where differing opinions and perspectives are rarely seen, and any bias potentially reinforced. So what does this all mean for brands? It means that trusted brands are more powerful than ever, as our 'go to' source of trusted information. It also means that a few missteps can destroy the trust in our brands that we have spent time and money building.

All organizations should therefore have an AI usage policy that lays out how they will and how they won't use AI, to make sure that all use of AI is done mindfully and carefully. These policies need to be reviewed and updated regularly.

However, beyond this policy, it is essential our organizations are investing in professional development to keep our teams skills up to date, so that they can understand both what is possible but also the implications of our use of AI.

I was very lucky to be invited to the UK House of Commons to take part in a debate about the use and regulation of AI. The below is taken from my opening statement:

> In the last seven days Goldman Sachs predicted that two thirds of jobs would be partially automated by AI over the next decade. British Telecom announced over 50,000 job cuts, of which more than 10,000 would be replaced by AI. Even OpenAI, the creators of ChatGPT, have told US Congress that AI needs regulation and could be highly dangerous without such regulation. In the last 24 hours the US stock market dipped because of an AI-generated fake image.

I went on to clarify that where the real danger lies, is if we do not continuously improve our skills and knowledge to help us use these tools effectively and to regulate them appropriately. Thankfully, our team won the debate.

A great starting point is to benchmark your own, and your teams skills, so we have created a skills benchmark that allows you to do just this, and is now the largest data-driven skills benchmark of its type globally: https://targetinternet.com/skills.

PART TWO
The digital toolkit

Introduction

This section explores a range of the digital tools and channels at your disposal in order to deliver your digital branding. This is the practical hands-on toolkit that will help you understand how the different digital channels fit together and are suited to impact different parts of the user journey, and to deliver your value proposition.

The guidance, tips and tools highlighted here have all been drawn from my own experience of planning and implementing digital campaigns for a wide range of organizations around the globe, from global film franchises through to chemicals that go into paint to make it whiter. The surprising thing is that most of these organizations have exactly the same problems and challenges. However, they may need to approach these challenges in slightly different ways, using different channels to achieve their desired outcomes.

In Part One we discussed the user journey; this section of the book is about selecting the most appropriate techniques to interface with that user journey in order to help create the value that we discussed.

We will also explore the idea of not making too many assumptions and making sure we always operate a 'test and learn' approach. A great example that I learnt through my own business demonstrates this well. I publish a regular digital marketing podcast, an audio show for marketers and business people generally, and as such it is a B2B podcast. As we all probably already know, generally speaking Facebook is not a place for B2B. As an experiment, we launched a Facebook page for the podcast to try to test if this assumption was correct. It took little resource as we basically used the platform to post links through to the content we were already creating and to generate some feedback on this content. We had little expectation but thought it a low-cost test worth a try.

The results were surprising, to say the least. We now have over 25,000 people who have followed the page, engaged with our content and drive traffic back to our website. This engagement drives signals back to Google, which in turn pushes us up the search rankings. I know of at least one very major project we have won because of the awareness this created, and it gives us a place for two-way dialogue with our audience.

Pragmatic curiosity

This section is a practical hands-on guide to using digital channels in the real world in a time-efficient way. However, it is also essential that we don't ignore potential options because of untested assumptions and that we don't become afraid of the new.

Digital marketing is generally moving at an incredible pace, and this is not going to slow down. It is very easy, and often sensible, to be suspicious of the never-ending flow of new channels and to adopt an 'I'll use it when it's been proven' approach. We do need to commit, however, to trying things out, albeit in a pragmatic and sensible fashion. In this section we explore how this is possible in practice.

> **LATEST TOOLS AND TECHNIQUES**
>
> Let's face it, by the time you read this there will be lots of new stuff that has happened between the time of writing and the book going to print. For that reason, I will be filtering and highlighting this latest news on the website that accompanies this book. I would also love your feedback and I'm also happy to publicize your efforts and experiences: https://targetinternet.com/resources/.

Social media 05

Social media has had the greatest impact on branding of any of the digital 'channels' we discuss in this section. Actually, calling social media a channel doesn't put it in perspective properly. Social media has fundamentally changed how we engage and interact with brands and has led to the fundamental shift in branding that this book is all about.

The fundamental shift is to that of two-way communications and empowerment of the consumer (in both B2C and B2B contexts). All of the topics we have discussed up until now, including the need for authenticity, clear value proposition and the increased complexity of the user journey, are all because of social media.

Through social media, rather than just broadcasting *at* you, I can engage *with* you. If you take any of the traditional branding metrics, such as awareness and recall – brand awareness is the extent to which a brand is recognized by potential customers; brand recall is when a brand is correctly associated with a particular product, branding or characteristic – they are far more likely to be impacted by 'engaging with' than they are by just 'looking at' something. However, engagement takes effort, so you first need to provide value in order to get them to engage. That value may take many forms, from entertaining through to educating (and potentially both at the same time), but you must give them an incentive to engage.

Social is personal

What we need to consider is how to best utilize this social behaviour for our organizations and to help achieve our business objectives, while providing value and without interrupting an individual's private and personal space. Only 6 per cent of people trust social media organizations (Thales, 2024), which indicates a general problem with how our data are used and how these social platforms are perceived as operating.

User journey and value proposition

Two of the main themes that we discussed in Part One were understanding the user journey and considering our value proposition. These considerations are key to using social media effectively. We need to make sure that we understand which social platforms our target audience is using and make sure that when they use these platforms the user experience provides value. Too much social media activity is carried out just for the sake of activity.

Content and engagement

Our ability to utilize social media effectively will come down to having interesting and useful content to share, and being willing and able to engage in an open and authentic way. Because of the personal nature of social media, a standard 'corporate communications' tone doesn't work. Even in a B2B environment, we are still dealing with individuals and need to apply core social media principles to our communications.

Bear in mind that anyone can blog or post to social media sites, but it doesn't mean anyone is listening. In fact, studies that look at how many times a day you should tweet suggest three times a day for some platforms (Macready, 2024). You should only do this, though, if you have something interesting to say three times a day!

Generative AI and content

A wide range of generative AI tools, from full platforms like OpenAI's ChatGPT and Google's Gemini, through to image specific platforms like MidJourney or audio platforms like ElevenLabs, all allow us to generate content in multiple formats. Whether it is the written word, synthesized speech, images, music or video, there are low-cost tools that now enable the easy creation of content. This has only added to the hugely noisy environment in which we operate, so making sure we use these tools to create content that actually provides value to our target audience is essential.

As well as considering the value our content is providing, we also need to make sure that we are aware of the copyright and usage rules around any content we use these tools to create. Each tool has its own set of rules, so it's essential we are aware of these so that we don't fall foul of any copyright and usage rules, or end up using content that our competitors can simply copy as we have no exclusivity.

Another consideration is style and tone of voice. Is the content we are creating with these tools actually in line with the rest of our brand? Many writing tools can effectively learn your brand tone of voice, but many image and video tools find it harder to follow your standard look and style (however, this is getting better).

Mobile social media experience

We need to consider the fact that the majority of people using social media on mobile devices are using apps to access these platforms. I personally use the YouTube, Facebook, X, Instagram and LinkedIn apps on my iPhone every day, as well as messaging apps like WhatsApp and content streaming like Spotify, which also has social functionality. So what does this particular way of accessing social media mean in terms of our digital branding? It means that we need to think in terms of accessing our content via the constraints of these apps and on these devices.

For example, if you post content to X, very often you will be sharing a link. How does that link display on a mobile device? With over 80 per cent of Twitter users accessing the service via mobile devices (WebFX, 2024), we need to consider the mobile experience of the links we are driving people through to. My own tweets with links split into two core categories: linking to useful content on my site and linking to useful content on other people's sites. I know that the experience on my site has been fully optimized for mobile users, but is this the case for other sites I am driving people through to?

Another example is using social networks such as Facebook and LinkedIn. Generally in this case we are posting content to try to create engagement, and very often this content will include images. The images may display very well on a desktop-size screen, but how do they look on a mobile? Much of the social network experience is different in a mobile app as opposed to a desktop version. We need to make sure we have considered this in all of our social posts. We have to assume that users will be on a mobile device at some point and therefore make sure that everything works in this format.

Informing your social media approach

Before we start any social media activity we need to start by listening. We need to understand what our audience is interested in and passionate about in order to inform our approach in providing value. In fact, social listening can help inform our digital branding overall, not just the social elements. There is a wide range of 'listening' or 'monitoring' tools, which will be discussed below. Understanding how someone searches can help inform our understanding of what their needs and interests are.

Using search to inform content themes

Google Trends is a fantastic free tool that allows us to see how users search in Google – and the trends that show over time. The great thing about this tool is that not only can we understand search trends but we can use this to inform our social content. We look at this tool in more detail in Chapter 6 (Search) and again when we look at judging the impact of our digital branding efforts (Chapter 12 Measuring digital branding), but here we use it to find out what people are interested in, in order to inform what we should be talking about on our social platforms.

In the screenshot shown in Figure 5.1, looking at the word 'jobs' we can start to see a clear seasonal trend. The peak in searches every year is in January, when many of us have new year resolutions and decide to look for a new job. This tapers off as we get back to work, and then many of us go on our summer vacation and get fired up again about looking for a new job. We then realize that Christmas is just around the corner and think we'll leave it to the new year. And this pattern carries on year after year! In the last four years, due to the global financial crisis, more people have been looking for jobs and therefore searching. Finally, we can see a huge increase in searches for 'jobs' in October 2011. Why? Because Steve Jobs (former CEO of Apple) died, and it creates a skew in our results because of the amount of people searching for his surname.

The Google Trends tool, as standard, will show you relative search volume over time for a particular word or phrase. We can drill down by time, region, country or language. The tool tries to identify related news stories at points on the graph, and shows us geographical interest and the most popular and fastest rising variations of these search terms. Probably the most important feature is the ability to compare the trends for different search terms, and this is particularly important for informing content.

Figure 5.1 Google Trends allows us to see volumes of searches for a particular phrase over time. This chart shows searches for the word 'jobs'

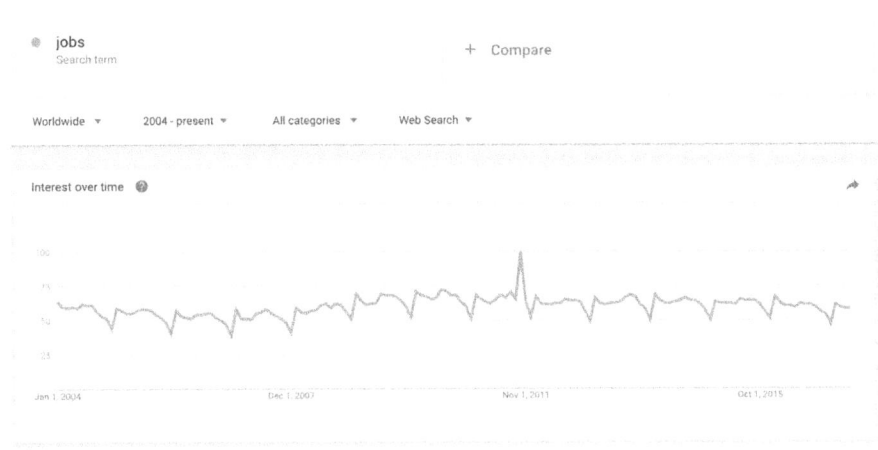

(Google and the Google logo are registered trademarks of Google Inc, used with permission)

Figure 5.2 Comparing words in Google Trends

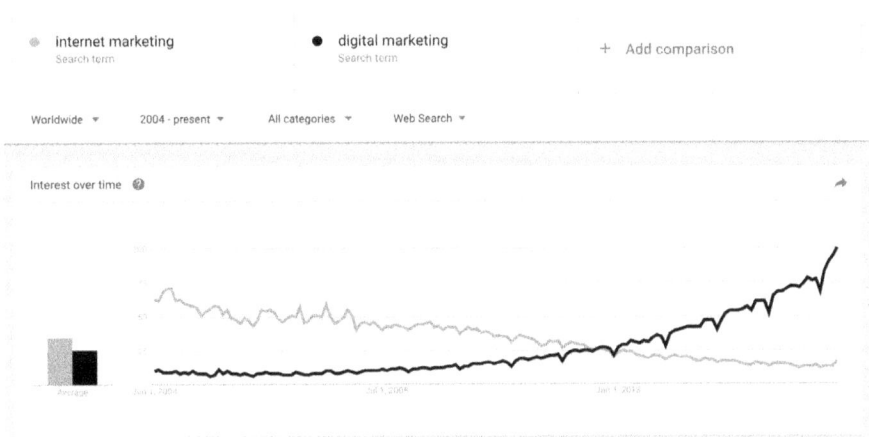

(Google and the Google logo are registered trademarks of Google Inc, used with permission)

Figure 5.2 shows the phrases 'internet marketing' and 'digital marketing' being compared. We can see a decline in interest for internet marketing and a rise in interest for digital marketing. I clearly need to be talking about digital marketing rather than internet marketing on my social platform, because that's what people are searching for and are interested in.

One thing to be clear on is that Google Trends shows you relative volumes of searches, not the actual numbers of searches. If you want the actual number of searches, you'll need to use the keyword planner (we discuss this in Chapter 6). Relative volume will show a word at a score of 100 at its highest volume of searches, and the rest of the score is relative to this. When multiple words are compared, the highest point given a 100 score is the most searched of the words being compared at its highest search volume.

One of the limitations of the Google Trends tool is its lack of ability to show trends for niche search terms. You'll find in many cases that a niche search term shows that it doesn't have enough data to plot a chart.

Social listening

Social listening tools are something that every organization of every size should be using. They allow you to monitor a number of different social channels to look for activity around certain phrases or topics. This capability can be used at a number of stages throughout social media campaigns, and they are an essential tool for effective social media use.

First, these tools can be used in the 'listening' stage, when you are trying to understand what social channels your audience is using, what they are saying, what they are interested in and what your competitors are doing. Many organizations will carry out a listening project before starting any social media activity, as part of their standard process before initiating a campaign.

Second, these tools can be used to monitor the effectiveness of our social media activity. We can monitor groups of words and phrases to see what is happening on an ongoing basis, and how our audience reacts to our social activity.

Finally, social listening tools can be used to manage outreach and engagement, by identifying key influencers on social channels. This can be important when trying to grow your audience but also when dealing with negative feedback or a crisis. The idea is to influence the influencers, much like in traditional PR, but in the case of social media we can do this at a much more granular level.

Some social listening tools also include elements of workflow management and help you to manage your social media efforts. For example, you may be able to track which social media users you have engaged with, which individual in your organization was involved and plan future activities.

Social media monitoring and listening tools

There is a huge array of social media monitoring tools out there, varying wildly in price and capability. At the free end of the spectrum you'll find a wide variety of tools. However, these tools are fairly limited, and the old adage that you get what you pay for generally holds true.

The amount of paid tools available is dizzying, but I would certainly recommend taking a look at the following:

- http://www.brandwatch.com – my favourite social monitoring tool and well worth the cost. Very powerful, flexible and used by some of the world's leading companies.
- http://www.mention.com – one of the lower-cost social monitoring tools with a free trial available.
- http://www.sproutsocial.com – essentially a paid social management tool, but it allows you to do some social monitoring activities.
- http://www.hootsuite.com – another social management tool that allows you to do some social monitoring activities, with a free version available.

Social analysis tools

Social analysis tools are different from social listening/monitoring tools in that they generally look at one social platform and give some analysis or functionality for that particular platform. In fact, many social media sites have these built in. For example, Facebook Insights will give you a range of reports that allow you to see which of your posts were most popular, where the users who like you are in the world and who is engaging with your content.

There are literally thousands of these tools out there. Generally they will analyse your audience and content and provide some insight into how to take your campaigns forward. I have highlighted a couple below to give a flavour of what you can expect:

- https://www.sparktoro.com – analyse social influencers with this excellent tool (see Figure 5.3).
- https://www.linkedin.com/sales/ssi – score your LinkedIn effectiveness using your Social Selling Index.
- https://www.upfluence.com/resources/influencer-search-tool – use this great extension to analyse influencer accounts and measure your own social success.
- https://www.fedica.com – advanced social analytics and influencer platform

The list could go on and on, so we've compiled and are constantly updating a huge list on the website to accompany this book. **Just Google 'Digital Marketing Toolkit' for the latest version.**

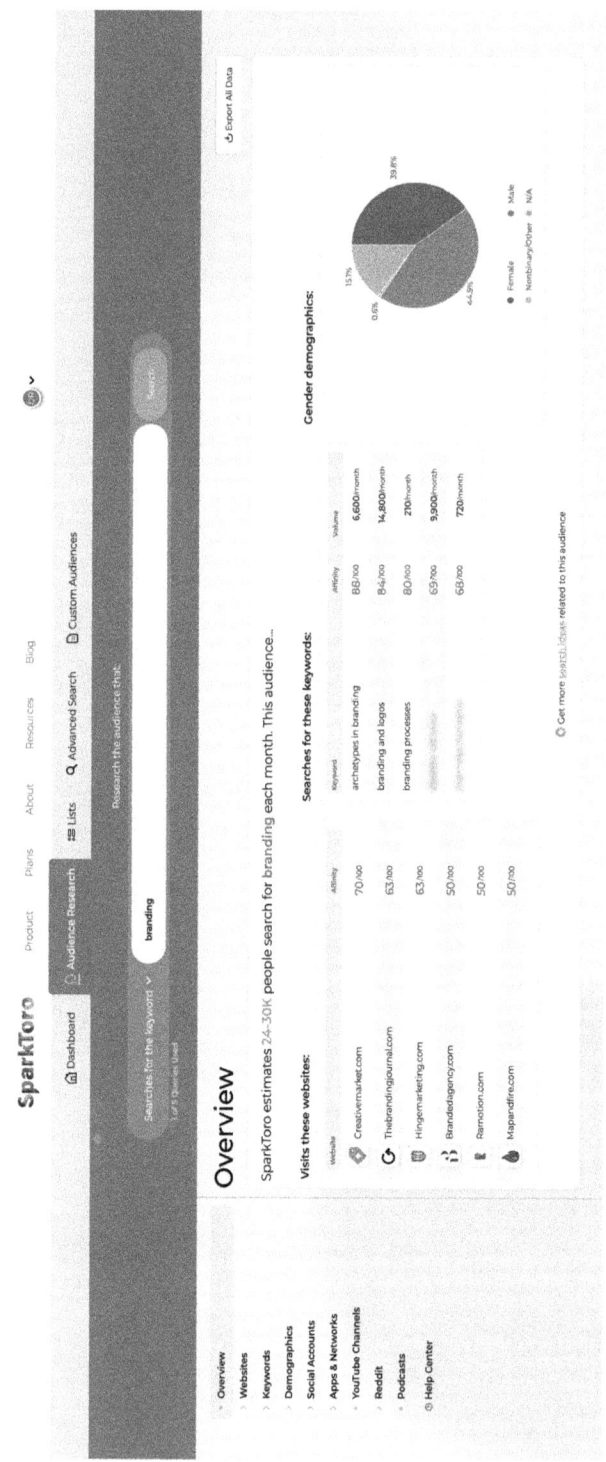

Figure 5.3 An example of the many social analysis tools out there and one of my favourites, SparkToro.com, looking at influential social accounts around the topic of branding

SOCIAL MEDIA IN CHINA

If you are targeting the huge potential of the Chinese market, or are working within China, you need to be aware (or probably already are) that social media in China can, on first sight, look very different from elsewhere in the world. Actually, the core principles of content, engagement and transparency all still apply, but you will find yourself using completely different platforms.

In most countries globally the social media platforms are fairly universal but in China there is no X, Instagram or YouTube; instead there are local market equivalents. TikTok is one of the few platforms to operate in China and across the rest of the world, but even this is under threat at the time of writing due to a potential ban in the US.

Just like any market, you need to understand what social platforms your target audience is using and then engage using the right tone and content.

For a great resource on social media in China, and the whole Asian region, take a look at: http://www.techinasia.com.

Analytics

Your web analytics is one of the most powerful tools for informing your social media activity. You'll not only be able to understand which social media sites are driving traffic to your website but also how many of these visitors are on mobile devices – and on which devices.

We will explore analytics in more detail in Part Three, but it is worth mentioning at this point that analytics can help you understand the impact of your social media campaigns on your broader digital objectives.

THE IMPORTANCE OF GOOGLE ANALYTICS

Google Analytics (and its latest incarnation Google Analytics 4 or GA4 as it is widely referred to) is a powerful and sophisticated web analytics platform that also happens to be free. It has around 89 per cent market share of the entire analytics market (6Sense, 2024) and is improving and offering more and more functionality all the time. It is suitable for the majority of site owners' needs and offers extensive reports around mobile sites and apps.

There are, of course, other commercial analytics packages available, and these have the advantage of account managers and Service Level Agreements (SLAs). Google Analytics 360 does offer these things, but pricing is currently US $150,000 per year.

Real-world integration

One of the greatest opportunities with any digital branding is to integrate multiple channels to work throughout each stage of the user journey. Social media gives us the opportunity to tie together online and offline experiences and merge them into more seamless experiences. We explore this idea in detail in Chapter 11 (From integration to transmedia campaigns).

Effectively implementing a social media policy

The internet is awash with social media disaster stories, and blog posts titled '10 social media fails' are almost certain to get lots of attention online. But

Figure 5.4 Word cloud of phrases mentioned online connected to social media disasters

Figure 5.5 Words used in association with social media disasters

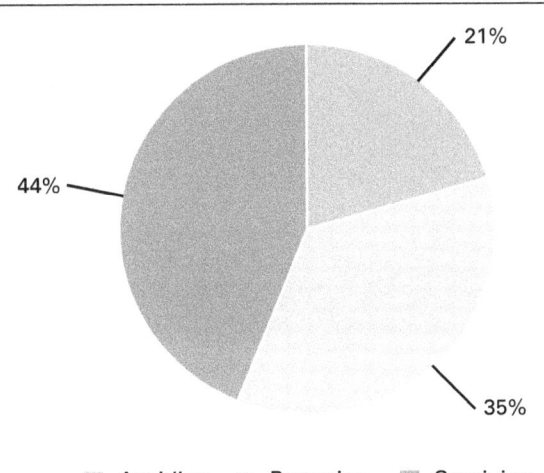

why do we like to see other people's disasters so much? Beyond the amusement value of some of the incredibly dumb things that people do, it's generally because the audience wants to learn how not to repeat the mistake. Figure 5.4 shows a word cloud (the bigger the word, the more times it was mentioned), showing the words and phrases that were mentioned online related to social media disasters (this was created using the fantastic https://www.brandwatch.com tool, which monitors millions of online sources such as social platforms, blogs and news sites).

So, many of us are searching for how to manage a social crisis, but it also seems that lots of us are searching for ways to avoid these things happening in the first place. Figure 5.5 breaks this down a little further.

Culture and process

So, it's pretty clear that not only do we need to try to avoid social media disasters, but we also need a realistic view that they do happen, and no level of preparation will allow you to avoid them completely. It's important to make it clear in your organization from the outset that although you can minimize problems occurring and you can fix them as quickly as possible by implementing the appropriate processes, you can't avoid them happening altogether. The world is a chaotic place and no one can predict the future, but we can implement processes that deal with the most common patterns

Figure 5.6 Peaks in interest caused by new articles being published giving advice on the topic

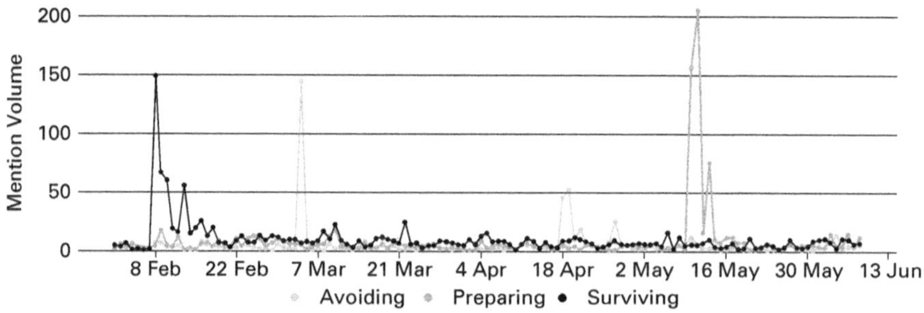

[Chart showing Mention Volume from 8 Feb to 13 Jun, with series: Avoiding, Preparing, Surviving]

in which problems occur and processes that help us avoid making the most common mistakes in the first place. We also need a culture that understands that building and iterating processes is essential and accepts that complete control is impossible. Culture is an important point to mention here as well because, as we can infer from the data below, the fear of social disasters is significant. Social media managers and marketers are very concerned about the impact these disasters can have on their companies but very importantly also on their careers. Figure 5.6 shows the number of mentions of avoiding, surviving and preparing for social media disasters. The spikes in mentions are not disasters happening and getting coverage, but rather a new article being published giving some form of guidance.

How to avoid a social media disaster

The key to avoiding social media disasters is process. Below are a series of steps that should be taken to allow social media to be carried out in the most risk-mitigated way possible. For some small and agile organizations, some of these steps may be overkill, but in any large organization a 'belt and braces' approach can pay dividends in the long term. Also, always bear in mind that social media itself is not normally the cause of a social disaster; it is more often to do with customer service or product problems, so make sure these teams are involved.

Panel sign off

Before anyone in the organization is able to start and undertake any social campaigns or activity, they must go through due diligence. This basically involves clearly documenting a series of answers to questions related to that activity. This would include, but not necessarily be limited to:

- What are the objectives of the activity?
- How will you resource the activity?
- What are the current topics of conversation in the topic area?
- What are our competitors doing in the area?
- Who are the influencers in the topic area?
- Do we have the appropriate tools in place for managing the activity?
- What happens if something goes wrong?
- What does going wrong look like?
- Have we brainstormed all of the possible disaster situations (see disaster prediction below)?
- Do we have an escalation policy and crisis management team?

It is also worth building a dialled down version of this process into any project of any type across the organization, so we are always asking the questions 'What are the social media risks?' and 'What could go wrong?' Once these questions have been answered, they are then reviewed by representatives from relevant parts of the organization. This normally includes representatives from marketing as well as legal/compliance. If the questions are not answered satisfactorily, the proposal is not accepted and must be revised and submitted again. If they are answered satisfactorily, the proposal is accepted and the team can go forwards and implement their plan, on the condition they do it within the bounds of the social media policy. This may sound laborious, but it does have an advantage for those wanting to implement their social plans. Once they have sign off, and as long as they adhere to the social policy, they don't need sign off for every post, tweet or response going forwards.

Social policy

Many social media policies simply list what we shouldn't do. They are lists of rules that either live in a drawer or on an intranet and are infrequently used. Although these policies should outline things we shouldn't do, they should also be a regularly updated guide to what we should do. By giving examples of things like tone of voice and examples of tweets that have been successful, a social media policy becomes useful and far more likely to be used.

> For examples of a wide range of other organizations' policies, take a look at: https://www.firmplay.com/social-media-policy/examples.

Disaster prediction

A very simple and effective part of your social process should be a brainstorming session. Get together as many people as you can comfortably fit in a meeting room and make sure you have a mix of roles, ages and seniorities if at all possible. Don't have too many senior people or anyone in front of whom others won't speak freely. You then ask everyone to brainstorm anything that could possibly go wrong with the social activity. Could the hashtag be hijacked and used for something else? Could the campaign be manipulated to communicate a message that wasn't intended? Is it just a dumb idea that people will laugh at? You need to let people be completely free to come up with pretty out-there ideas.

The next stage is to filter what you have come up with. You then put the whole list to an anonymous vote, allowing people to indicate if the risks identified are possible (or simply ludicrous) and the perceived likelihood that they could happen. Any deemed to be completely unlikely are discarded. Those that remain then have responses planned for them. If someone hijacks your hashtag, what do you do? Stop using it? Respond? In each case you need a planned mechanism to either fix or contain the problem (more on this in the crisis management section).

Social listening

Every social project should start with a listening project. This will allow you to understand what the popular themes of content are, who the influencers are and should also help you to identify any potential risks. You can also look at what your competitors are up to and set some expectations of the level of engagement you'd like to achieve. You'll need a decent social listening/monitoring tool. You start by creating a set of words that you want to look at, and the better tools give you a query builder to do this. You can see an example query in Figure 5.7 that monitors a whole range of words but also excludes some word combinations.

Figure 5.7 Building a query for social media listening

Staff training

All staff should be trained in your social media policy, and this should form part of your induction. They should then get updates on a regular basis to either improve their knowledge or just to remind them of the key issues. This way people know what is expected of them, what they should and shouldn't do, and what the processes and tools available are.

Ongoing monitoring

Once you start a campaign or any social activity, you then need ongoing social media monitoring tools. These will allow you to gauge the reaction to your efforts, monitor your competitors easily, identify influencers and, most importantly for our purposes, identify any issues very quickly. The better tools will automatically create alerts for you that flag up any change that is statistically significant without you needing to look for it (Figure 5.8).

Clear responsibilities

You need to clarify from the outset who is in charge of monitoring and reporting on social media. What happens when they are not around? Who takes over? Who is responsible for dealing with customer complaints that

Figure 5.8 Email alerts for topics that are growing quickly (screenshot of Brandwatch's 'Signals' system)

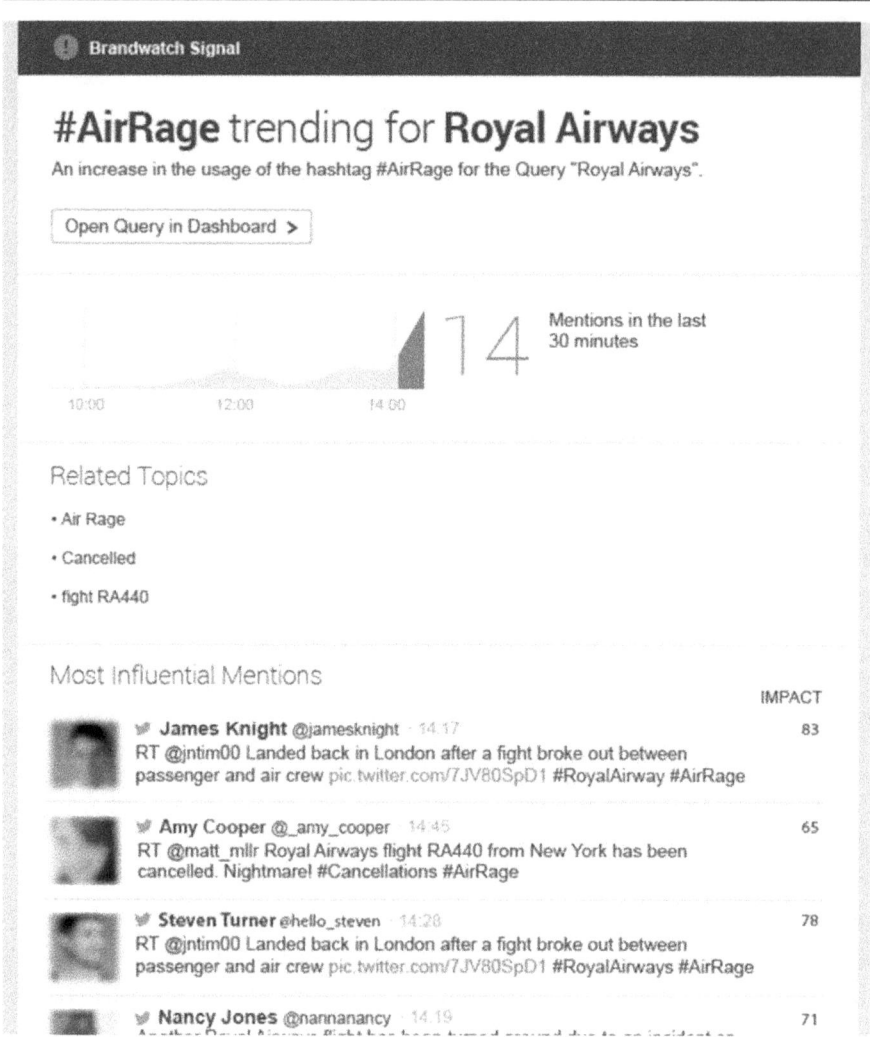

come in via social media? How quickly should they be responded to? How quickly should your internal legal or compliance team turn things around? All of these activities and more need to be clearly documented and expectations for different roles and teams made clear. Very often internal SLAs are a good idea in large organizations, so that different departments and teams are clear on what the expectations are.

Response tracking

Once you start getting responses to your social activity, you will need to respond to many of these (whether negative or positive). The more successful you become at social media, the more of these responses you will get, and this is when you will need a tool to help you. It is important that you track things like complaints and you respond to compliments, and make sure they are assigned to the right person and tracked through to completion. There is a range of tools available but two of my favourites are Hootsuite and SproutSocial.

> **VIEWPOINTS**
> Sarah Dawley, Head of Content, Hootsuite
>
> **The new conversational customer journey**
>
> With almost two decades under its belt, social media has matured into a staple of almost every marketing and communications campaign. And with the ever-expanding plethora of paid advertising options, social media has also evolved into a powerful, reach-oriented marketing channel that is eating up considerable amounts of marketing budgets as well.
>
> As brands raced to stay connected with customers during the pandemic, their spending on social media skyrocketed. The CMO Survey UK (2021) found that social media spending increased from 13.3 per cent of marketing budgets in February 2020 to 23.2 per cent in June 2020 – a whopping 74 per cent lift. And that spending is expected to remain stable for at least the foreseeable future.
>
> Because of that, social media has become a fiercely competitive place for brands. And that competition is leading to a lot of bad habits: spraying and praying, running from one social network to the next, frantically pumping out content to grab any morsel of attention possible.
>
> At Hootsuite we often get asked: 'What's the secret?' How do we get more attention, more shares, more likes, more engagement? There is, of course, no secret formula. (Sorry.) But after helping brands succeed on social for more than 12 years now, we've seen clearly that the brands who win more often than not are those who prioritize conversations just as much as conversions or clicks. Those who haven't lost sight of social media's most potent attribute (and biggest opportunity): the ability to listen and

engage, to have instantaneous two-way interaction and to nurture relationships.

Conversations build trust, add value and make people feel heard and appreciated. But on social, they're also an important way for brands to provide emotional – not just functional – fulfilment at any stage of the buying journey. And emotions are what bind customers to brands.

The idea of conversation is also what's at the heart of today's modern consumer expectations: instantaneous, cross-channel, personalized attention and care. Discovering a new product from a brand's post on Facebook, buying it on Instagram, reaching out with an issue on Twitter, following up via email and leaving a review on Google. Customers are well accustomed to the entire buying journey now taking place entirely upon these two-way, conversational platforms.

But it's not just customers who benefit when a brand prioritizes two-way interaction and conversations with customers at scale, instead of simply using these platforms to broadcast message after message to anyone (or no one). Today's top marketers know that both participating *and* listening to conversations on social can generate invaluable insights and intelligence that can be used to actually *enhance* the customer experience.

This is what brands and modern digital marketers need to aim for: using conversations on social media to build relationships focused on legitimate customer needs, not just their own self-serving goals of popularity or profitability. It might not be a secret formula, but it's certainly a recipe for success.

Escalation process

Once something is identified as a potential issue, it is essential there are clear guidelines for what happens next. Who needs to be told? Via what channel? How quickly? It's no good sending me an email on Friday afternoon if I'm not checking my emails until Monday morning. There needs to be a clear process for flagging up potential issues to the right people and a fallback process for when they are not available. We also need to define what a problem looks like and who is responsible for deciding when something is becoming a problem.

Crisis management team

Once we've decided something is becoming an issue (and it's sensible to be pretty cautious in your approach – better to escalate something that blows over than ignoring something that explodes into a crisis!), we need to have a nominated crisis management team. This team will be removed from their day-to-day roles and put onto dealing with the issue head on. Therefore, we also need to plan what will happen to their normal workloads.

Social media crisis management plan

This is the process that should be initiated once things have been handed to the crisis management team.

Speed of response

Most social media disasters happen because organizations are paralysed by fear and a lack of planned responses. It can then take too long for a response to be signed off and things escalate. Our aim is to respond to any issue as quickly as possible in a measured way. We therefore need to answer these questions as quickly as possible: Do we have any pre-planned responses from our disaster prediction process? If so, are they fully suitable? If so, have they been signed off for usage?

If we have no pre-planned response we need to create a response. Normally an honest and open tone is appropriate, not a corporate 'don't admit any liability' tone. Taking responsibility where an issue is our fault and suggesting a resolution is desirable. Always be cautious if the resolution could be seen as insufficient for the problem that has occurred. Better to make a gesture of goodwill than to be seen as uncaring.

Once the response is created, we need sign off as soon as possible. The crisis team should have immediate access to and prioritization of their requests by the person who is able to sign off the response.

Not responding

Bear in mind that sometimes no response can be the best response. If a serial complainer is complaining again, even though you responded positively previously, you may make a decision to ignore the complaint/comment. Audiences are quick to identify serial complainers and often, if you respond, you simply give them a platform from which to escalate things further. However, ignoring a complaint or comment should only be done as a conscious decision and still requires sign off.

An alternative approach to not responding at all is to respond via a third party. For example, if we previously identified advocates, that is people who are positively inclined toward us and are likely to say positive things, we may ask them to join the conversation. Telling people what to say on your behalf can backfire, so we are simply asking them to join the conversation. Always remember, though, that an overzealous advocate can also make things worse, so it's important you trust how this individual will act.

Monitoring reaction

Once the response is issued, we need to see how the audience reacts. Very often involving advocates at this stage can also help as they can amplify and share our response. Be prepared for your response to either get no traction or to not get the desired impact. In this case we loop back to preparing further responses and involving advocates again.

Holding patterns

Very often, particularly in large organizations or when dealing with legally sensitive issues, we can't issue a full response immediately. In these cases it is essential to issue a holding response and to set expectations. For example, we may say that we are aware of the issue and that while we carry out some internal investigation, we can't respond in full, but that we will issue a full response by a defined deadline. These kinds of holding responses can help to minimize rumour and escalation before our final response. It makes sense to always have a holding response prepared and signed off in advance so these can be issued as quickly as possible. Holding responses should be carefully crafted so they are not seen as admissions of guilt or cause any other forms of further escalation. It is worth putting your holding response through a disaster prediction process, as discussed earlier, as well.

Post-crisis debrief and social policy update

Once the disaster has been averted or passed, we then need to make sure it doesn't happen again. The crisis team should debrief the relevant teams and then amend the social media policy to add additional advice and learnings. All staff should then be briefed/trained on the change.

Social crisis management conclusions

The majority of social disasters can be avoided by following a series of processes that we have identified, but bear in mind, the majority of social disasters are not caused by social activity. Normally social disasters are caused by issues like customer service or product faults. Therefore, the responsibility for preventing disasters lies across the organization and all staff need awareness and training.

When social disasters do occur, we need well-prepared crisis management teams and processes to minimize the damage and give a response as quickly as possible.

Outreach, engagement and ego

To really get the most from our digital branding, we should always consider how we can maximize our reach into our target audience. Social outreach and engagement is a highly effective way of doing this, and as well as increasing the size of our audience, it can help us to create positive engagement.

If I keep on publishing useful and engaging content, regularly update my social channels and positively engage with anyone who leaves comments or feedback, I will gradually grow my social media audience. If, however, I want to speed up this process and create the maximum amplification for my efforts, then I am going to need to focus on social media outreach.

Social media outreach is all about identifying the key influencers and advocates within a particular group. If I can get these key people to share my updates and content then I can amplify my visibility and potentially grow my audience.

So let's define what we mean by an influencer or an advocate.

Advocates are the easiest group to identify as they are those people who leave positive comments, re-tweet things and generally engage in a positive way. They are willing to spread what you say and add to your social voice. They are our greatest asset and we need to engage, encourage and reward this group in order to build loyalty.

Figure 5.9 Upfluence is a social media influence scoring platform

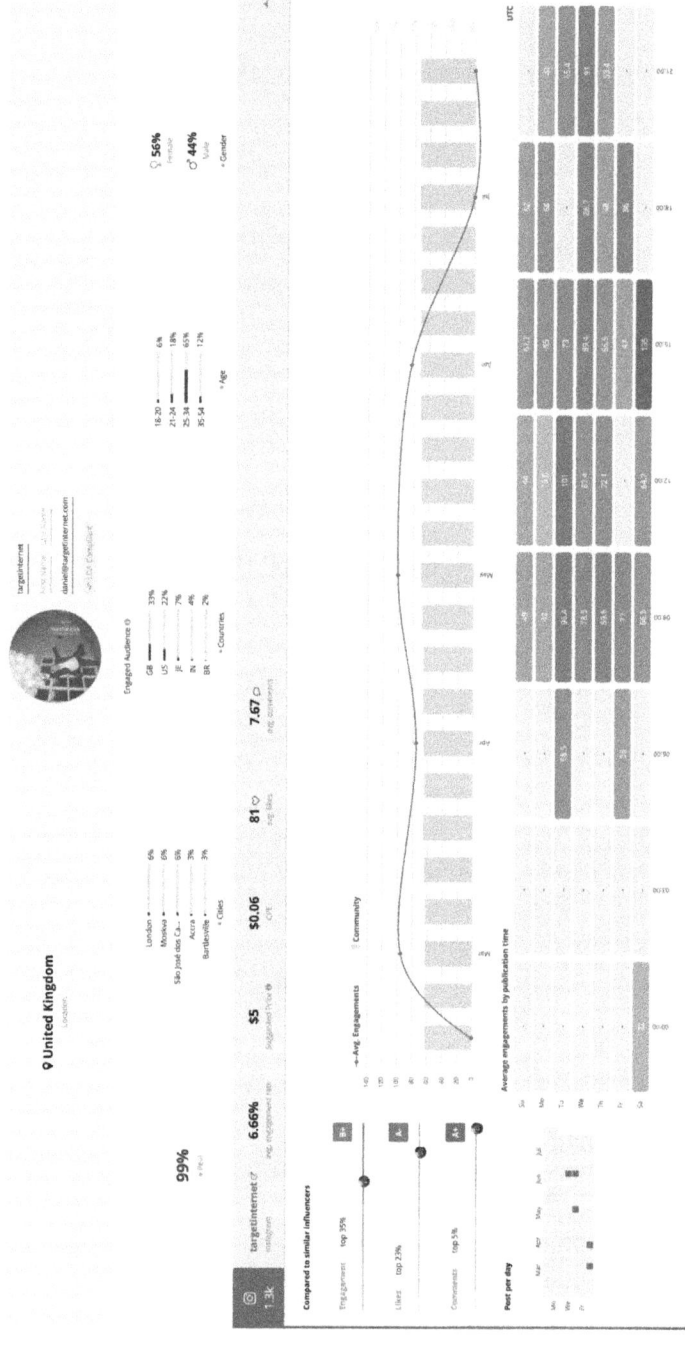

Influencers are those people with access to the audience that we want to influence. We can use social media tools to identify them and we then need a strategy to get engagement and encourage them to become advocates.

Judging influence

You can use a number of measures to judge influence online. You could look at the number of social connections that someone has, or look at the quality of their audience. You could consider how likely it is that what they say will be read and repeated. This process can be quite time-consuming and therefore it is worth considering some of the key tools that can help us understand influence.

Upfluence (and in this case their free Chrome extension), shown in Figure 5.9, aims to take the pain away from trying to work out influence online. I've gone to my Twitter profile page and then clicked on the Upfluence Chrome Extension. The extension has used my Twitter profile to look up all of my social accounts, score me against other influencers and identify my best performing social posts.

Scoring services such as Upfluence all judge influence differently and then have algorithms that take into account a wide range of factors. There will always be arguments about how much a particular factor or platform should be weighted, but in reality it can give you the rough guidance you need. If I look at all of my Twitter followers and look at those with the highest Upfluence scores, there is no doubt that these people are my most influential audience.

We can use these platforms to assess our own accounts, benchmark against competitors and identify influencers. The key point of tools like Upfluence is that they provide nice easy metrics and visualizations to initially assess influence – you can then dig a little deeper and plan your outreach campaigns.

Another approach to judging social influence is to use a social monitoring tool that helps you to identify the most influential accounts on a particular topic. We mentioned the tool **SparkToro.com** earlier, and it is excellent for identifying influential accounts on a particular topic.

BRAND, SOCIAL MEDIA, ONLINE PR AND SEARCH OPTIMIZATION

It is important to understand that there is a very close connection between your social media activity, public relations (PR) activity and search optimization. It is also essential to realize that all of these things make up a significant part of your digital branding. We will look at search in more detail in the next chapter, but the effectiveness of your social media activity will create 'social signals' that influence your search rankings (essential to the quantity and quality of conversation that is happening in social media around your topics of interest).

Social engagement and outreach are essentially online PR, but your offline PR activities can also impact what you talk about in social media and how many people are linking to your sites and social media platforms. For this reason, we need everyone involved in these three disciplines to be working collaboratively and be aware of what each other is doing.

Social measurement

The greatest mistake made in a huge number of organizations (in my experience, the majority) is to focus on volume-based metrics when looking at social media campaigns. More often than not, a campaign is started and the initial target is to reach a certain number of likes or followers. But, in reality, what does having a million followers actually mean? The answer is actually very little. We need to understand who that audience is, look at how engaged they are, their sentiment and, most importantly, understand if social media is actually having an impact on your business objectives.

Part Three looks at analytics and measurement in much more detail, but we can use analytics in a number of ways to look at the success of our social media effects. We can start with the basics and look at how much traffic we get from social media sites to our websites. We could then take it a stage further and look at how many of these visits are on mobile devices. If you are using analytics effectively, you also will have set up goals, and you can see what part social media is playing in driving your website visitors to complete your goals. All of this will be covered in more detail in Part Three, but the key point to remember here is that it's not just about the social media data, such as number of followers or amount of engagement – it is actually about understanding how this drives your end objectives.

Sentiment analysis

Many social media tools will carry out some form of sentiment analysis. The idea is that the context of the social media mentions that you receive is analysed, and the sentiment or intention of the social media user is understood. This most usually takes the form of grouping these mentions into positive, negative and neutral.

There is a problem, however. The majority of social media tools get this completely wrong. These tools work by analysing the text and using fairly rudimentary methods of analysing the language. For example, if I tweet 'Top 10 digital marketing disasters of 2025' and then link to my website, many tools will see this as a negative tweet and associate negativity with the link to my website. It will be seen as negative due to the use of the word 'disaster', even though from experience I know that this will actually be a very popular tweet. Some tools, however, are a lot more effective at analysing language and take a far more sophisticated approach. These tools certainly aren't 100 per cent accurate, but they are far less likely to make rudimentary mistakes like this.

The solution is to understand how effective your particular tool is at analysing the social platforms you are looking at, and then manually checking the results you get. This doesn't mean reading every single tweet or comment (although in an ideal world you will), but it certainly means scanning through and understanding the assumption that the tool is making.

This is particularly important when you look at 'share of voice' (a measure that we look at in detail in Part Three). During a really bad social media crisis, when everyone is talking about you and saying negative things, your share of voice will be high. You therefore need to understand sentiment when you look at share of voice.

Social media advertising

Many social media platforms give you a number of paid advertising options. Major search engines such as Google, Bing and Baidu also allow you to run paid search campaigns (discussed in more depth in Chapter 6). We need to discuss the implications of paid social campaigns here, however, as they can heavily impact the effectiveness and measurement of your social campaigns.

Value proposition, privacy and trust

Since social media is very much part of our personal lives in many cases, we need to be very cautious about how we use it in a commercial way. Almost everything we have spoken about so far involves providing value via engagement and understanding the user's needs. Exactly the same principle should be applied to social media advertising.

We need to consider how much of an interruption social advertising can actually be seen as, how it can actually damage our brands if used badly and what image of our organization we are projecting.

The key point is to understand the social platforms you are using, why a user is there and to make sure that the value proposition is clear. If you are on Facebook and you are interested in health and fitness, and a brand such as Nike offers you free tools to help you achieve your fitness goals, then that's great. If, however, you are on Facebook and you have liked a digital marketing podcast, it doesn't mean that any of your friends necessarily have an interest.

Trusting algorithms

It is actually in Instagram's interest not to annoy people with irrelevant ads, just as it is not good for Google to give you irrelevant search results. Both scenarios lead to dissatisfied users, which in turn leads to those users moving to other social networks and search engines.

The algorithms – which are just sets of rules and logic – behind these sites are what decide on what ads you are shown or what search results you are given. Google has spent many years and much investment in developing its algorithms and focusing on relevancy. The Facebook algorithm filters out content that it thinks isn't relevant to the user and reorders other content based on how relevant it appears to be. However, it also means that Facebook is able to sell advertising due to organizations not necessarily being able to get their content in front of their audience for free. 'Organic reach' is the consequence of this algorithm, and your organic reach is the percentage of people who have liked your page on Facebook who actually see your content. The average organic reach for a wide range of organizations is currently 1 per cent or less. This basically means that so few people who have liked your page actually see your content, you need to pay for additional visibility.

Social media conclusions

As well as needing to consider all of the usual complexities of social media when planning our digital branding, we have some additional things to take into account. We still need to consider appropriate use of channels, focus on content and engagement, and find effective measurement strategies. Most importantly with digital branding, we need to consider the overall user experience and be very clearly focused on transparency and trust.

The overall user experience is all down to making sure we have thought through and tested how the user will actually experience our social media content and how they can engage with us. Although time-consuming and fragmented, due to the number of social platforms and scenarios involved, it is a very practical and reasonably straightforward issue.

Trust, on the other hand, is far more subjective but is of huge importance. Social media can act as a magnifier for missteps we make as marketers. By interrupting, being irrelevant or making incorrect assumptions we will actually inconvenience our target audience. This may be by giving them irrelevant content to scroll past, or bombarding them with the same message again and again.

Social media is at the heart of what makes digital branding so special – and it carries both risk and opportunity. A well-planned and strategic approach to social media will not only make best use of the tools and channels available, but will do so with a view on how this makes up part of the broader user journey.

Search   06

Search is a fundamental part of the user journey. What we search for – and the results that we find – have a massive impact on our digital branding. Making sure we understand what our target audience is searching for at different stages of the user journey will be essential in order to deliver the best user experience. If we can't be found, or if we drive our audience through to a poor user experience, we will damage our digital branding. The best website in the world is useless if it can't be found.

We would normally divide search into two key areas: 1) natural (or organic) search, the area of the search results decided upon by the search engines; and 2) paid search, the set of results that we can pay to be visible in. Search engine optimization (SEO) is the process of achieving search rankings within the natural/organic results. Pay per click (PPC) refers to the paid search element of search results. We explore both in this chapter.

Let's start by giving an example of how search tools can demonstrate the importance of search as part of our digital branding. Figures 6.1 and 6.2 are screenshots from Google Trends, a fantastic tool that we explore later in this chapter. These two screenshots show the reaction to a TV campaign in regard to users doing search.

Enter the drumming gorilla

Nearly 20 years ago, Cadbury, the confectionery manufacturer, released a viral TV campaign. This involved a very intense scene of a gorilla listening to music and then playing the drums along to the music. The music in question was 'In the Air Tonight' by Phil Collins, and if you haven't seen this ad then go and search for 'drumming gorilla ad' on YouTube.

This was the first ad of its type and it caused a huge amount of conversation, mainly because people had no idea what a gorilla playing the drums had to do with Cadbury's chocolate. The answer is very little, but this randomness was the campaign's genius. So what did people do when they saw the ad? They did a search on Google.

Figure 6.1 Searches in Google for 'drumming gorilla'

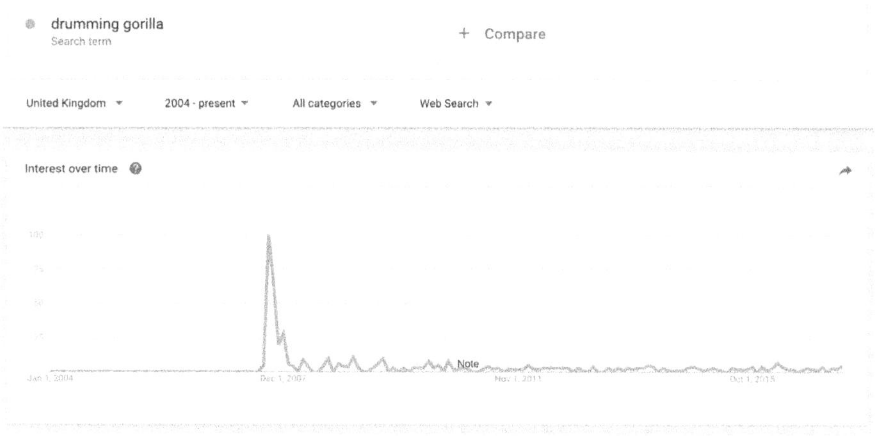

(Google and the Google logo are registered trademarks of Google Inc, used with permission)

Figure 6.1 shows that there were no searches for drumming gorillas on Google until the ad came out (not all that surprising), but when it did there was a spike in searches for this term.

However, Figure 6.2 shows that people actually searched for 'cadburys', meaning that the brand experience was going to be massively impacted by search. This shows that we need to anticipate the target audience's reaction to every channel that we use and realize that even traditional broadcast channels are now, and have been for decades, impacted massively by our digital branding.

SEM – MY LEAST FAVOURITE THREE-LETTER ACRONYM

As you have probably already worked out, we love three-letter acronyms in digital marketing. Of all these acronyms, SEM is my least favourite. It stands for search engine marketing, and technically speaking (I'll happily argue until I'm blue in the face over this) it means both sides of search marketing – that is, both SEO and PPC. However, it is often used to describe the paid side of search, PPC.

Figure 6.2 Searches in Google for 'drumming gorilla' and 'cadburys'

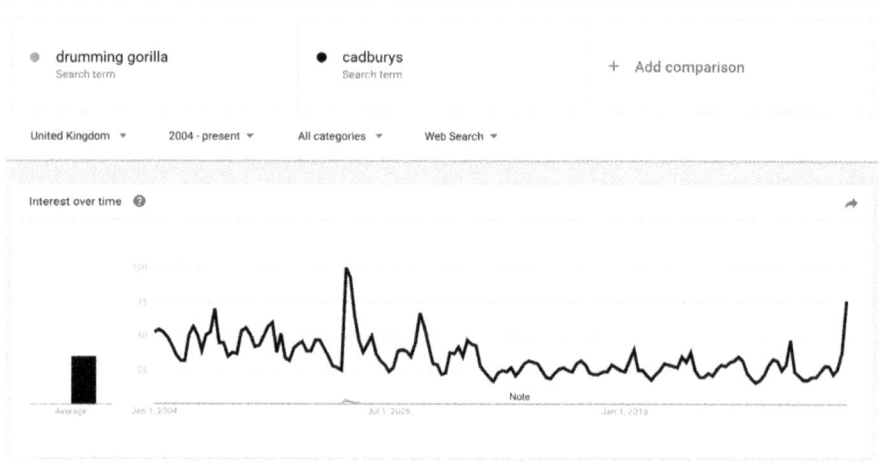

(Google and the Google logo are registered trademarks of Google Inc, used with permission)

In reality, we could place PPC in the advertising section of this book, because that's exactly what it is, a form of paid advertising. However, the term 'online advertising' is most often used to refer to banner and video ads, so for the sake of consistency with this definition, we will discuss PPC within this section of the book.

THE PPC/SEO RELATIONSHIP

There has always been discussion and rumour around how much your SEO results are boosted by spending money on PPC campaigns. The answer, for the vast majority of search engines, including Google, is that there is no direct correlation whatsoever. I have had clients spending millions of pounds every month, and there was no direct impact on their natural search rankings. This rule, however, doesn't follow for Baidu, the largest search engine in China. Fundamentally, the more you are spending with Baidu the better your natural search visibility tends to be. It's a nice easy way to get search rankings, but probably not the best way to give the user the most relevant search results.

Search engine optimization

SEO is all about getting to the top of the search engine results in the organic results. Thankfully, the core rules of SEO are consistent across all major search engines, and we will explore those core concepts here. We also look at how the user journey impacts search and what we need in order to maximize its positive impact on our digital branding.

It all starts with spiders

Spiders are bits of software that read your pages and send the content back to the search engines. If they can't read your site, you won't get rankings.

The search engine spiders (also known as crawlers, bots or robots) visit your website, follow the links on your pages and send your content back to the search engine so it can then be assessed and ranked. These data that have been sent back to the search engines and have been assessed are known as the search engine index. Generally, the more often you update your content, and the more important your website is seen to be (we'll cover this 'importance' later in the chapter when we look at link building), the more often the spiders will come back to look at your content.

There are certain practices that can stop the spiders from reading your content in the first place and, clearly, if your website can't be read, you won't get ranked. For example, if everything is behind a login, Google can't see your content. Another common problem is putting text in images. Google spiders just see a 'lump' of image and don't see the text within it. Although images can have Alt tags that describe them (these are edited in the code of your site or by using your Content Management System), this never gets as much weighting as actual words on the page.

> **MOBILE SEARCH**
>
> Starting in 2019 and fully rolled out in 2021, Google moved to mobile first indexing. That is, Google reads the mobile version of your website to decide what shows in Google. This means that Google is extremely keen for us to give users a good experience not only on desktop but also on mobile devices. We discuss this more in Chapter 7, but it is worth remembering that any site that gives a poor mobile user experience is likely to be 'punished' by showing lower down the search rankings. Make sure your website is mobile friendly by using the Bing Mobile Friendly test: https://www.bing.com/webmaster/tools/mobile-friendliness.

Google operators

If you want to check that Google is visiting your website and when the spiders last visited, you can use the following technique, known as a Google operator. Go to Google as normal, but instead of searching for a word or phrase, type the following into the search box (of course substituting 'your-website' for your own domain name): cache: **www.yourwebsite.com**.

This will bring back a copy of your website and some details that tell you when Google last visited your site. If this returns nothing it may mean that Google is not visiting your website.

Google Search Console

For some real insight into how Google's spiders are accessing your pages and any problems they may be having, you need to use Google Search Console. You can find the Search Console here: **https://search.google.com/search-console**.

You will need a Google account to set things up (you can set one up in a couple of minutes), and you will then need to prove that you own the website you want to get some details on. Google provides step-by-step instructions, but you will need to be able to either edit your web page's code or to create a new page with a specific name (as this demonstrates to Google that you control the website). Existing Google analytics users can avoid these steps by just connecting the two accounts.

Once installed, Google Search Console allows you to do the following:

- **Get Google's view of your site and diagnose problems:** you can see how Google crawls and indexes your site and learn about specific problems they are having in accessing it – probably the most important feature in regard to what we have been talking about.
- **Discover your link and query traffic:** you can view and download data about internal and external links to your site with the link reporting tools, find out which Google search words/phrases drive traffic to your site and see exactly how users arrive there.
- **Share information about your site:** this allows you to tell Google about your pages with Sitemaps, which pages are the most important to you and how often they change.

Core Web Vitals

Google rolled out a new site of 'tests' in 2021 and updated with some new tests in 2024, referred to as Core Web Vitals. These all relate to giving a good user experience. Essentially Google wants your web pages to load quickly, for a user to be able to interact quickly and for things not to 'shift' about once they have loaded. If you don't meet these standards your search rankings may suffer due to providing a poor user experience, so review your results and get a developer to review things if you are scoring poorly.

AI content and SEO

Google came out several years ago, before the widespread usage of generative artificial intelligence (AI) tools, and warned website owners that using AI-generated content would lead to them being punished in the search rankings. Then, in 2023 they made a statement that completely changed this position and stated that AI-generated content was a valid way of creating content, and that great content was great content, however it was created. The key point here is 'great content'. If you use AI to create huge amounts of low-value content, you will be punished in the search ranking. Not necessarily because Google will directly punish you, but rather because of all of the poor user 'signals' this will generate. People leaving your website quickly, not engaging with your content, not scrolling and so on, all tell Google that you content isn't meeting users' expectations. You can read Google's full guidance on AI-generated and assisted content here: https://developers.google.com/search/blog/2023/02/google-search-and-ai-content.

EEAT

In response to AI-generated content, as well as other forms of low-quality content, Google issued its EEAT guidelines. This stands for:

- Expertise;
- Experience;
- Authoritativeness;
- Trust.

Essentially, by demonstrating these qualities, your content is deemed to be worth ranking. So we can use AI to help generate content, but we should do things like including examples, case studies, images, audio, video, quotes and so on to demonstrate our expertise and experience. The website that the content is published on as well as the author are assessed for their authority on the subject and overall this all builds trust.

Well structured, researched and carefully crafted content, that is based on helping serve the needs of our target audience, naturally tends to have the qualities of EEAT. If you focus on creating 'helpful, reliable, people first content' you will provide all of the signals that Google is looking for via your highly engaged website visitors.

> **GOOGLE SEARCH GUIDE**
>
> Google has just updated its excellent SEO Starter Guide. Even though it is titled as a starter guide, there is plenty of insight contained in its pages for even experience SEO practitioners: https://developers.google.com/search/docs.

Keyword research for SEO

Keyword research is all about understanding how our potential audience searches so that we know what search phrases we need to rank for. Once we have done this we need to look at getting the words onto our pages (we will cover this below when we discuss on-page optimization).

It is too easy to make assumptions about what words and phrases our potential audience is searching for, based on our own opinions (or possibly the opinions of our search agency). We need to back this up with real facts, and happily there are plenty of free tools that allow us to do just this.

Keyword challenges

Some of the everyday challenges you will face in keyword research are best demonstrated by giving an example. When I ran a search agency we had a large recruitment client whose basic brief was: 'We want to be number one for the word "jobs".' What they were basically asking for was to be number one out of about 18.7 billion pages. We did it (and they are still in the top five), but was this worth the effort and cost?

Generic search terms

Achieving number one positions for broad and generic search terms like this just won't be achievable for most of us (at least in the short term). We won't have the resources (financial or time based) to achieve this. In reality, we would also be wasting a lot of time. Who actually searches for the word 'jobs'? It is most likely to be someone who is assessing the marketplace of recruitment websites. They are at the browsing stage of the online journey and are probably fairly unlikely to be applying for a job on this first visit. In reality, if we start by saying 'I want to be number one for "digital marketing jobs London"', then we start to target people nearer the point of conversion (when they are actually going to do something), and we will be competing against much fewer people (5.5 million in this particular case, which is a lot better than billions!).

So why would a large organization like the recruitment website I mentioned go for such a generic search term? There are a few reasons outlined below:

- Ignorance – they may not know very much about SEO.
- Long term – it is valid to approach more generic terms in the long term. It is achievable if you are willing to keep working at it, and it can make up part of a mixed keyword strategy (this is when you target lots of phrases in lots of combinations on a certain topic).
- Volume – if you sell online advertising you may be more interested in volume than quality. This is because online ads are generally sold CPM (cost per mille or, basically, cost per 1,000 views). The more pages seen, the more money you make, regardless of whether or not the visitor was interested or relevant.

Long tail search

The majority of searches have three or more words (SEMRush, 2024). The more specific the phrase we search on, the clearer we are on what we are looking for and the more likely a search is to lead to an action. Some form of action, such as a purchase, download, application, etc is what we generally want to achieve as marketers, so these longer, or long tail, phrases are what we should often focus on. The phrase 'long tail' comes from the idea that there is a wide selection of search phrases made up of multiple words that will not drive huge volume (although using multiple long tail phrases can drive lots of traffic) but are more likely to drive conversion (the completion of an online goal such as download, purchase or a form being filled in).

Keyword variations

We also need to understand exactly how people search, and the order and variations of words that they use. Google wants to match exactly what you search for, so the difference between 'Jobs Manchester' and 'Manchester Jobs' is important. Which variation do most people search on? Luckily, Google provides tools that can tell us exactly this – the two key tools are discussed below.

Keywords Everywhere (https://keywordseverywhere.com)

Keywords Everywhere is an extension for the Google Chrome browser that gives us data on each of the searches that we do in Google. The tool shows us search volume, average cost per click for pay per click ads and relative competition level between 0 and 1 (1 being the most competitive, meaning the phrases that most people are trying to get to number one in the search rankings for). The tool also shows trends over time and its integration into Google Search makes it very easy to use, as you can see in Figure 6.3.

It's not a free tool, but it's very low cost and you pay US $18 for 100,000 credits. Each time you do a search it uses around 30 credits because it looks up the phrase you search for, and also looks up all of the related phrases as we can see here.

Google Trends (http://www.google.com/trends)

Google Trends can tell us quite a lot about how people search, but its key capability is in showing trends over time and comparing search terms. Enter a search term and it will show you the trend over time of people searching for that term. It doesn't show an actual number of searches but rather the trend (the keyword planner tells us actual numbers). We can also enter multiple terms and see how they compare. Its other key capabilities are to show geographical interest in a term by country, which can then be drilled down to by region and city. Always remember that when two countries are compared, it is showing where somebody is more likely to be searching, not necessarily that there is actually a larger volume of searches in that country. Finally, we get a selection of other words that have been searched for in relation to this term, which are the most popular and which have grown most in the past year.

The screenshot in Figure 6.4 shows a comparison of the search terms 'blackberry', 'nokia' and 'iphone' in the UK market. We can see a direct correlation between the market for these brands and the volume of searches for them. Also remember that bad news stories, such as the 'Blackberry Blackout', when the Blackberry network stopped working for a number of days, will also cause a peak in searches.

SEO, local search and Google Business Profile

Local search is hugely important, and maps can dominate the search results for some types of searches. For this reason we need to maximize our opportunities of getting listed on these map-based results. Bing, Yahoo, Baidu and Google all allow you to list your location on a map via their mapping

Figure 6.3   Keyword volumes using Keywords Everywhere

Search terms		Avg. monthly searches	Suggested bid	Add to plan
digital branding		2,900	£3.22	

Keyword (by relevance)		Avg. monthly searches	Suggested bid	Add to plan
brand marketing		9,900	£3.03	
online branding		1,900	£0.98	
digital branding agency		320	£6.51	
digital brand marketing		70	£6.68	
brand advertising		2,900	£1.02	
email marketing		74,000	£11.79	
digital branding company		210	£4.92	
web design		301,000	£5.35	

(Google and the Google logo are registered trademarks of Google Inc, used with permission)

Figure 6.4 Google Trends comparing search terms

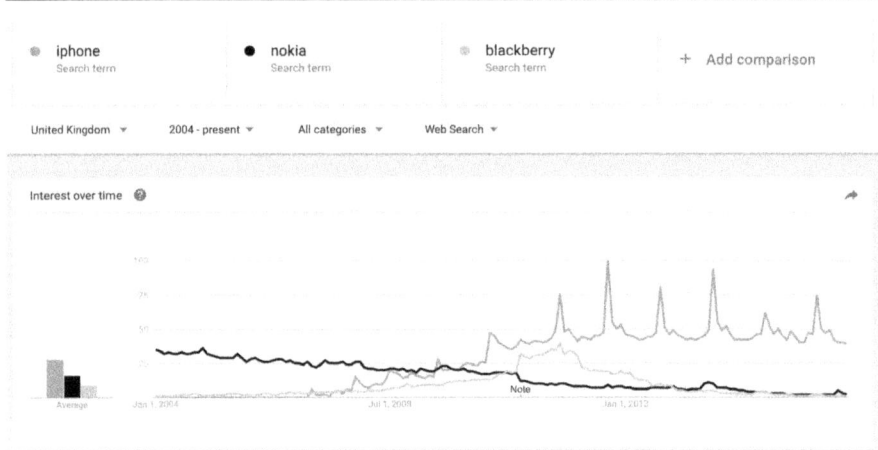

(Google and the Google logo are registered trademarks of Google Inc, used with permission)

services. The more detail you can add to these map-based listings the better, and generally by connecting these listings to your website (which all of these search engines allow you to do) you stand a better chance of showing up in the map results in a mobile search.

Google offers a specific service to add any business with a physical location to Google's index. You Google Business Profile allows you to enter your map location and other attributes such as opening times. You can set up your profile here: https://www.google.com/business/.

On-page optimization

So far we have explored the topics of search engine spiders and keyword research. This means we have made sure that the search spiders can access our web pages and we have identified the words that we want to achieve rankings for. The next stage is to get these words onto our pages. On-page optimization is all about getting the right words on the page, in the right place. We have identified the right words during the keyword research phase, and now we need to put them in the right places. This is a fairly straightforward process and is just a matter of looking at the core elements of a page and factoring in our words and phrases.

> **USERS FIRST, THEN SEARCH ENGINES**
>
> What we are trying to do is help the search engines understand the content on our web pages. However, we don't want to do this at the expense of the user journey. What I mean is that if we over-optimize our content it will make our copy hard to read. You can drive all the traffic in the world, but if everyone leaves when they start trying to read your content, you've wasted your time. Focus on getting things right for the user first and then we will adapt things as appropriate for the search engines.

I have listed below the key areas of the page that are of most importance. We will then look at each of these elements in more detail:

- page title;
- headings;
- web page names;
- copy;
- link text;
- file names;
- alt text.

Each of these different parts of our web pages give us the opportunity to show the search engines what our web pages are all about (see Figure 6.5). So let's take a look at them in a bit more detail.

Page title

This is the most important thing on the page, as it is generally given the greatest weighting by the search engines and it is what actually shows up in many search engines (including Google) as the main title in the search engine results pages (SERP – see Figure 6.6).

The page title is actually something that shows up in the top bar or tab of your browser window, and is something that most users don't even notice. It is something that is initially written by your web developer or content management system (CMS), and is one of the most commonly missed and most effective elements of SEO. Huge numbers of website page titles are blank or say things such as 'Home'. In other cases people repeat the same

Figure 6.5 The key elements of the page involved in SEO

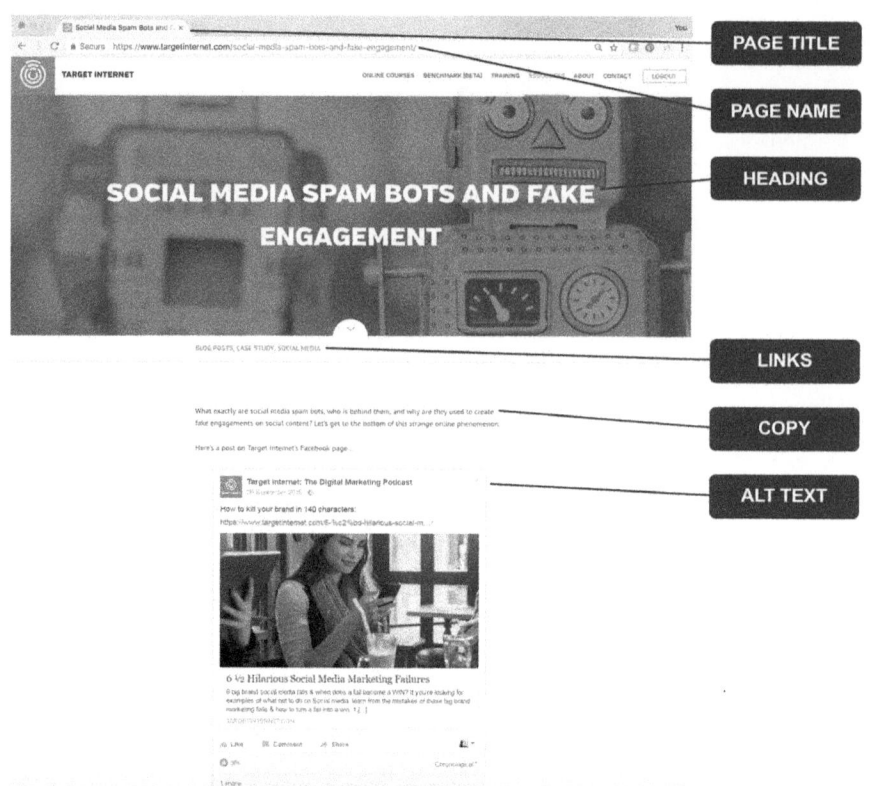

Figure 6.6 The page title is the main line of the search result in Google

Social Media Spam Bots and Fake Engagement | Target Internet
https://www.targetinternet.com/social-media-spam-bots-and-fake-engagement/ ▾
What exactly are **social media spam bots**, who is behind them, and why are they used to create fake engagements on social content? Let's get to the bottom of ...

(Google and the Google logo are registered trademarks of Google Inc, used with permission)

page title again and again, or use their company name. If I am looking for your company name then that is fine, but what about when I am searching for what you do? A good page title factors in a range of phrases that a user may search for.

So, for example, 'Online Digital Marketing Training from Target Internet' is a much better page title than 'Target Internet', as it says what my site offers and includes the words and phrases that a user might search for.

Headings

The headings and subheadings throughout your pages help the search engines to understand the key themes of these pages. Again, these should factor in the most important words and phrases that a user may be searching for and that you have identified during your keyword research.

The spiders are reading the code of your pages. The headings in your copy are represented as H tags. These are part of the HTML code that goes into building your pages, and you have up to six different tiers of heading tags. The H1 tag is your main heading; the H2 tag is for subheadings and so on all the way through to H6. In reality, we most often don't get past using H1s and H2s, which is absolutely fine from an SEO perspective. It is important to understand, though, that you should only ever have one H1 but you can have multiple H2s. The logic behind having only one H1 is so that you are clearly indicating the core theme of your page. Multiple H1s would water down this core theme and make it harder for the search engines to understand the real focus of your page. This is a common mistake and should be avoided.

Bear in mind that the actual part of your page that is used as an H1, H2, etc will be decided by either the person who originally coded your page or the CMS that you are using. For this reason it may be necessary to have the code of your pages modified to use the appropriate part of the page as heading tags. Thankfully, in systems such as WordPress this is all taken care of for you in a very sensible way.

Web page names

Your website address and the actual names of the pages that you create will again act as indicators for the search engines as to what your content is about. This doesn't mean your website name must include your keywords, but it does mean that you should name your pages appropriately. For example, my website doesn't have to be called http://www.digitalbranding.com if that is the topic of the content (although in an ideal world it would be), but if I create a page on this topic I should name it www.mywebsite.com/digital-branding – this is because the search engines are realistic in realizing that many of the addresses for our sites are our company names and so on. Again, this may be impacted by your original developer or CMS, and systems such as WordPress help you to control this easily.

Copy

The main copy on your pages should include your targeted key phrases, ideally in the first paragraph. However, you certainly don't need to keep repeating the words again and again. In fact, if you do repeat the words again and again, not only can you make the copy hard to read, it could actually be interpreted as negative by the search engines.

> **ETHICAL SEO**
>
> What we are talking about here is ethical SEO. This means we are trying to help the search engines to understand our content. We could also try and manipulate the search engines. If you get caught using manipulative techniques, you can get completely removed from some search engine results, and Google is particularly effective at detecting these techniques. The main rule is that the website content should be there for the user and not the search engines and that what the user is shown is what the spiders should also see. If you want to understand more about what Google expects and considers to be best practice, take a look at their webmaster guidelines: **http://www.google.com/webmasters**.

Link text

The words that we link on within our webpages help the search engine to understand the relevance of the page we are linking to (they also to some extent help set the context of the page we are linking from). The words we are using to link are referred to as anchor text, and they are an important indicator for the search engines. For this reason we should not use phrases such as 'click here' or 'read more' as these are essentially meaningless to the search engines. These types of phrases also make it harder for a user scanning your page to quickly identify its core themes.

File names

Although only a small factor, the names of the files that make up your pages have some impact on the search engine's understanding of your pages. So you should name your images, video files and so on appropriately to describe their content and, where possible, to factor in your keywords and phrases.

Alt text

Alt text is text that describes an image and is put in place by a developer or using a CMS. The alt text is there for accessibility reasons primarily but also has an impact on SEO. Accessibility is all about making your website usable for people who need to use it in a different way for some reason. For example, if I am a blind user, in order to use the web I will use something called a screen reader, a piece of software that reads out web pages in a simulated voice. When this reader gets to an image, it doesn't understand it, so it reads out the alt text instead. The search engines have a similar problem with images. For this reason they read the alt text in order to better understand the image.

As I said above, the alt text is for accessibility, and SEO should be a secondary consideration. However, if you can factor your keywords and phrases into these descriptions, it does help with your overall SEO efforts. You should also be aware that effective use of alt text is very important and is a legal requirement within the European Union under the Disability Discrimination Act. Wherever you are based, however, alt tags are important to help people access your website, and they have an impact on SEO.

On-page optimization in perspective

Once you have been through the process of identifying your most important words and phrases, and made sure they have been put within your pages in the appropriate places, you have done the fundamentals of on-page optimization. The search engines get smarter and smarter about understanding how different topics and themes are interconnected, and Google in particular is getting very good at understanding the context, as well as words, of a particular piece of content. For this reason, you should not obsess too much over on-page optimization, but rather focus on providing value through content. That leads us into the extremely important next step in SEO.

Link building

If on-page optimization is telling the search engines what your content is about, link building is telling the search engines the authority of that content. A link to your content from another website is basically seen as a vote of confidence. People only link to content they find useful or interesting, and links are therefore essential to your search optimization efforts.

Neither on-page optimization nor link building can work in isolation, as both are needed in order to understand the topic and authority of your site and its content. Driving more links to increase your authority is all about creating engaging and interesting content, and this is one of the reasons why 'content marketing' has become such an important approach in recent years. If our websites just say how great we are or how great our product is, there is little reason for anyone to link to us. However, if we provide value via our content, we are encouraging links, building value and potentially driving engagement.

Social signals

As well as looking at the number of links to our content from other websites, the search engines are increasingly concerned with what we call 'social signals'. These social signals are the conversations that are happening in social media about your site and content. This is not to say that you can tweet about your own site a thousand times, however, and that you will suddenly leap to the top of the search rankings! Recall in Chapter 5 that we looked at the social scoring service Upfluence, which attempts to score the social influence of a particular user or social media account. In reality, the major search engines have an internal process that works in a similar way, and they are trying to access both the quantity and quality of social signals that are being created about your content.

This increasingly means that using social media to get users discussing, engaging with and sharing your content is highly important.

User behaviour

As well as looking at the words on our pages, how many people are linking to our websites from other sites and how many people are talking about us in social media, Google also heavily weights user behaviour.

So for example, if you click on a search result, and then quickly go back to the Google results, that is a negative signal for Google. It indicates that I haven't found what I'm looking for.

Another example of user behaviour impacting search results is when I click on the second place results rather than the number one listing. When I read the page title in blue and the description underneath, I may decide that the result lower down the page looks more relevant to me. If enough users do this, eventually the result in 2nd place will be pushed up to first place because of Google recognizing this behaviour.

Google also consider dwell time, that is, how long you actually spend on a page. So by creating content that engages your users and keeps them on your pages, you are signalling to Google the value of your content and helping your search rankings.

Measuring link authority

There are a number of tools and methods for measuring how effective our link-building strategies are and how authoritative our sites are seen as being. All of these are looking at two key things: the quality and quantity of links and social signals to our content.

> **SEARCH ENGINE ALGORITHMS**
>
> Much of what SEO agencies concern themselves with is understanding the algorithms that the search engines use to decide how your content is ranked in the search results. In my opinion, this is increasingly a waste of time. The smarter the search engines get, the more complex their algorithms become and the more of a nonsense it becomes trying to decode this set of rules. I was told by someone at Google that in reality, even within Google, there would be only a handful of people who know and understand the complete set of rules, because it is such a complicated and huge thing. Rather than focusing on trying to outwit the engineers at Google (good luck with that!), we should focus on the fundamental issue of creating useful and engaging content.

Link Explorer

This is an excellent tool from Moz – moz.com offers a huge range of SEO tools as part of their paid monthly subscription. You can also access Link Explorer in a limited way for free. It doesn't give you all of the features, results are limited and you can use it only 10 times in a month, but it is still fantastically useful (see Figure 6.7). When you enter a website or particular

The digital toolkit

Figure 6.7 The excellent Link Explorer from Moz

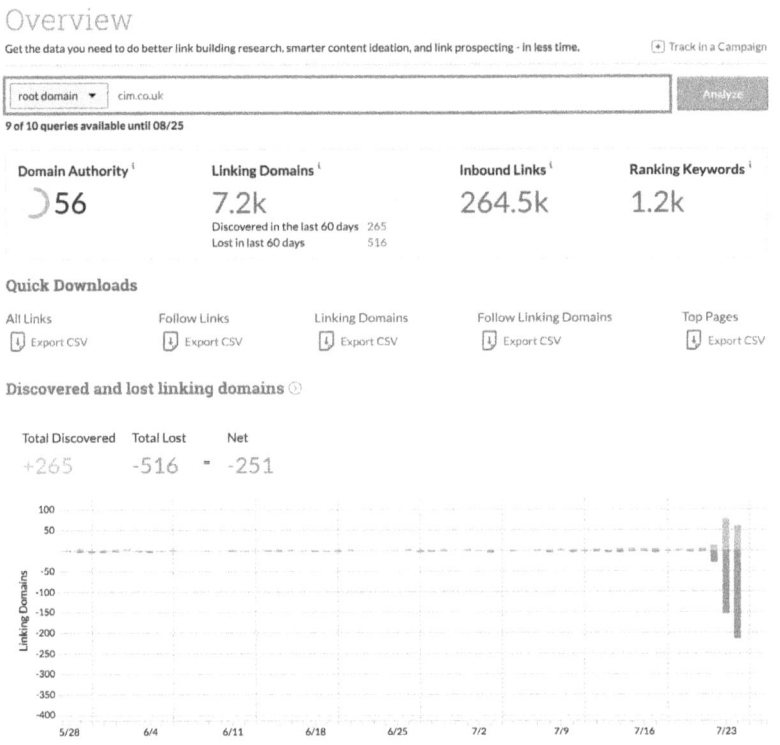

web page into the tool it gives you a range of information about the quantity and quality of links to that page. You are given a score out of 100 for the authority of your domain as well as any particular page you are looking at. It's a great way of benchmarking yourself, and you can do the same for your competitors.

SEO summary

We can sum up SEO into some fairly straightforward key steps:

- User journey – understand what your target audience may be searching for and why. Make sure you understand the user journey and know how search fits in.
- Spiders – make sure that my content is visible to the search engines.

- Keyword research – understand what my target audience is searching for and build a list of words and phrases that I would like to rank.
- On-page optimization – get these words on my page in the right places.
- Link building – build a content-based strategy to encourage links to and discussions around my content.
- Social signals – post and promote my content on social media.
- User behaviour – make sure my content is engaging and provides value.
- Benchmarking – measure and improve my SEO efforts.

Paid search

PPC is the other side of search. We will look at the pros and cons of PPC in detail, but its key advantage is our ability to control and target it precisely.

So how does paid search fit in with branding? It is not about display; that is, it is not the fact that your ad shows up and, even though people don't click on it, it has an impact on your branding by being seen. This is about direct response and driving your audience through to relevant content at an appropriate stage in the user journey. The experience of finding what they are looking for – the experience of what your content offers – is what impacts your digital branding.

If you receive a promise of number one rankings in search from an agency or freelancer, one of two things is happening. They are either talking about PPC, or they are lying. No one can guarantee you number one rankings on Google, even someone who has done it a thousand times before, because only Google control it (see Figure 6.8).

Another major advantage of PPC is speed. You can be number one in the search rankings almost immediately if you are willing to pay for it. Organic search can take months to achieve rankings for competitive terms, and even then it is not guaranteed. Also, don't mistake organic search for being free. Although you don't pay for every click, you will spend time and effort creating content and so on.

PPC is an auction-based system. The more you are willing to pay per click, the more visibility your ad will generally get, although the quality and relevance of your ad will also impact your ads visibility. This also means that the more competitive your particular industry is, and the words that you choose to target, the more expensive it can become. More on this later in this chapter.

Figure 6.8 Paid search in action in Google

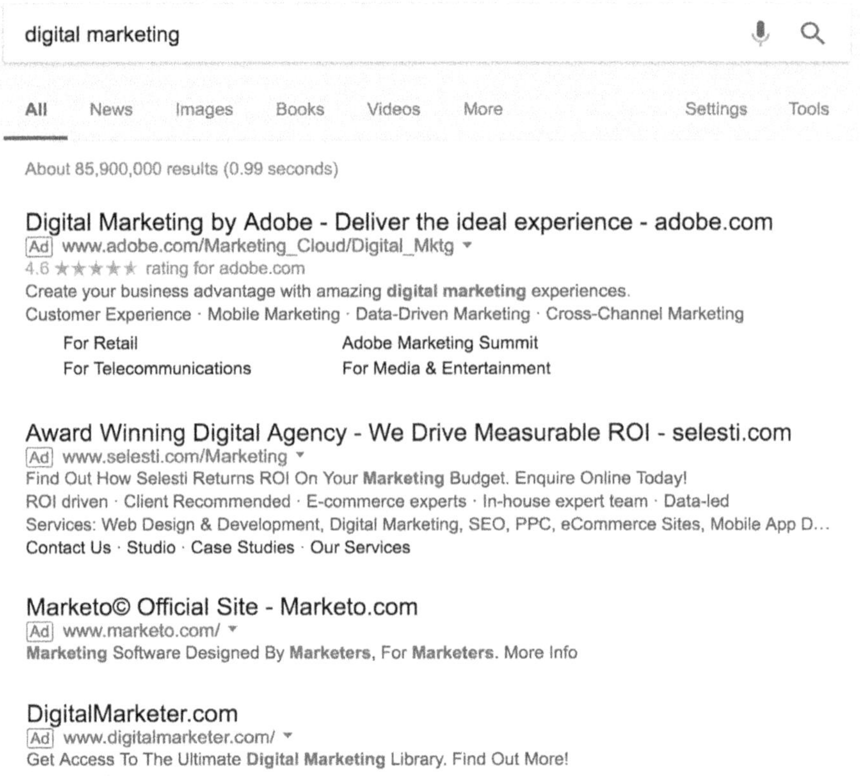

```
digital marketing                                              🎤  🔍

All    News    Images    Books    Videos    More           Settings   Tools
───

About 85,900,000 results (0.99 seconds)
```

Digital Marketing by Adobe - Deliver the ideal experience - adobe.com
[Ad] www.adobe.com/Marketing_Cloud/Digital_Mktg ▼
4.6 ★★★★★ rating for adobe.com
Create your business advantage with amazing **digital marketing** experiences.
Customer Experience · Mobile Marketing · Data-Driven Marketing · Cross-Channel Marketing

    For Retail   Adobe Marketing Summit
    For Telecommunications   For Media & Entertainment

Award Winning Digital Agency - We Drive Measurable ROI - selesti.com
[Ad] www.selesti.com/Marketing ▼
Find Out How Selesti Returns ROI On Your **Marketing** Budget. Enquire Online Today!
ROI driven · Client Recommended · E-commerce experts · In-house expert team · Data-led
Services: Web Design & Development, Digital Marketing, SEO, PPC, eCommerce Sites, Mobile App D…
Contact Us · Studio · Case Studies · Our Services

Marketo© Official Site - Marketo.com
[Ad] www.marketo.com/ ▼
Marketing Software Designed By **Marketers**, For **Marketers**. More Info

DigitalMarketer.com
[Ad] www.digitalmarketer.com/ ▼
Get Access To The Ultimate **Digital Marketing** Library. Find Out More!

(Google and the Google logo are registered trademarks of Google Inc, used with permission)

PPC fundamentals

The key steps involved in planning and implementing a successful PPC campaign are:

- set objectives;
- keyword research;
- create ad copy;
- select additional ad features;
- set targeting criteria;
- set budgets and bids.

Set objectives

Since the introduction of Google Analytics 4 (GA4), Google Ads uses the 'Key Events' you have set up as your campaign objectives, and these are used by the machine learning in the background to optimize your campaign for success. Key Events are simply the desired outcomes that you have set up in Google Analytics, such as an ecommerce sales or a lead form being filled in. However if you don't have these GA4 key events set up, you won't get the most out of Google Ads. At the outset of setting up your PPC ad, you select one or more of the Key Events you have set up to be your campaign objective/s.

PPC keyword research

There will certainly be commonality between this and the keyword research you do for your SEO campaigns, and you will use the same tools. However, one fundamental to understand about PPC is that the more precise your selection of words, and the better matched these are to your ad copy and landing pages, the more successful your campaign will be.

The words you select for your PPC campaigns will trigger your ads. You could select a generic search term to trigger your ad so that you get lots of traffic. This is a very good way to spend lots of money and get little result. You could also use lots of different search terms to trigger the same generic ad. Again, a good way to waste your budget. Generally, a very specific key phrase that triggers a specific ad, and which sends the searcher to a very specific and relevant landing page, will get the most from your budget.

Create ad copy

Fundamentally, a PPC ad is made up of a number of lines of text and a link through to your site (or a number of links). This copy is what grabs the searcher's attention and attracts the click through to your site. We won't go into copywriting techniques here, as much has been written on the topic already, but the wording of your ads needs to reflect the right context.

Bear in mind that most paid search platforms, including Google Ads, now use machine learning to help show the right ads to the right people. For this reason, these platforms will ask for multiple versions of your headlines, descriptions, calls to action and so on, and then mix these different assets to show different ads to different people. The machine learning-based optimization will then learn what asset combinations work best, by optimizing for your desired outcome that you set at the objectives stage.

Additional ad features

Google (and Baidu) offers a number of additional ad options to enhance your PPC ads. An example in Google is that you can include links to multiple pages of your website. You can also add to your ads links to maps of your location.

These additional ad features serve two purposes. First, they clearly encourage users to take an action in response to your ads. Second, they can make your ad more likely to be noticed in the first place as they differentiate your ad visually and generally add to its overall size.

Set targeting criteria

You can target by location-based criteria. Location-based targeting is split into three key areas in Google (most other systems follow similar principles, although accuracy can be poor in Baidu in particular):

- targeting by physical location in which the search is made (eg searching for 'hotels' while in New York);
- targeting by what people are searching for (eg searching for 'hotels in New York');
- targeting by intent – this is based on various factors that Google consider, such as previous searches (eg searching for 'hotels' after having searched 'trip to New York' and 'best deals flights New York').

Set budgets and bids

As well as setting your daily budget (the maximum you are willing to spend each day) you can set your maximum cost per click (CPC) or cost per acquisition (CPA). CPC/CPA is the main factor that decides where your ad shows up on the page. Because PPC systems generally work on an auction basis, the more you are willing to pay per click, the higher up the page your ad appears and the more visibility it has. That visibility should lead to clicks, assuming your ad content is appealing to the searcher. You should not assume, however, that it is always better to be in the top positions on the page. You may find that being further down the page means you are paying less per click and getting clicks more slowly, but you get better value overall from your budget. This is one of the many reasons that in order to get the maximum value from your budget you need to test and adjust your campaigns on an ongoing basis.

CPC/CPA can be set at a number of different levels. You can apply a single maximum CPC to a group of ads or just for a particular key phrase. Many systems, including Google, have an automatic bidding option that will try to maximize the number of clicks you receive for your budget. Just remember, though, that the maximum volume of traffic does not necessarily mean the maximum amount of conversions on your site.

Within Google Ads you also have the option to set rules-based bidding, meaning that you do things like automatically adjust your bid (within a certain range) to always keep your ad in a certain position. This can help you to automate your bidding in order to factor in changes in competition levels.

PPC considerations

Beyond the fundamentals of PPC, there are some other things we need to consider when planning our campaigns that can have a significant impact on what value we get for our budgets.

Ongoing management and optimization

To get the most out of your PPC budgets your campaigns will need to be closely monitored, tested and adjusted on an ongoing basis. Levels of competition can change, and bids will need to change accordingly. You may find that certain keywords are working well and that others, although driving traffic, are not converting into business. Again, you will need to adjust your campaigns accordingly. This means that as well as considering the cost of your PPC budgets you need to factor in the time or cost of managing your campaigns effectively (we will discuss below using agencies for PPC management).

Quality scoring and ad rank

The Google Adwords system is particularly focused on rewarding campaigns that are highly targeted and give relevant results to searchers. They do this by factoring in a quality score when deciding what ads to show and how high up the page those ads should be displayed. Quality score takes into account a number of factors but looks at things like the click-through rate (CTR) of your ad in order to signify its relevance. This means that ads that are seen as being relevant are given a boost in their positioning, and you can actually have your ad appearing above someone else's who is actually paying more per click than you.

Other quality factors include having the word/phrase that was searched for actually in your ad and on the landing page that you are sending searchers through to.

Your quality score is combined with other factors, such as how much you are bidding and the expected impact of the ad format you use, to give you an overall 'Ad Rank'. This Ad Rank decides where your ad shows up.

The more relevant your ad, the better your quality score and the more visibility you get for your budget. It also means that Google is rewarding relevant ads, which in turn means that searchers see PPC ads as more relevant generally, and thus should in turn click on the ads more, thus making Google more money. Clever stuff.

Conversion tracking

As with any digital marketing activity, we need to understand what impact it is having on our bottom line. We will discuss the idea of a 'conversion' further in Chapter 14 (The role of analytics), but most PPC systems give you some ability to track beyond a click and see what happens afterwards. After all, all the traffic in the world is useless if the visitors to your site all leave immediately upon arrival.

Working with PPC agencies

Agencies can help you get the most from your PPC budgets by planning and setting up your campaigns effectively and then managing your campaigns on an ongoing basis. They can also add additional cost but bring little benefit. If you plan to work with an agency you need to be very clear on what value they provide and if this is giving you a positive ROI.

From my experience of working with lots of agencies, and having run a search agency, there are a couple of key things to look out for:

- **Payment terms** – far too many PPC agencies charge on percentage of spend basis. So, for example, you pay them 20 per cent of what you are spending on your PPC clicks. This approach makes no sense, for a couple of reasons. First, more money does not necessarily mean more work to manage that budget. It may do, but it is really down to how that budget is being spent. Second, as an agency there is no incentive to save you money and reduce your budget – if that is then going to reduce the agency's fee.

- Another issue to consider is **campaign ownership and handover fees**. What I mean by this is to be very careful of contracts with PPC agencies that state they own the campaign data and/or that there is a handover fee for your campaign. This can mean that you are charged to set up a campaign, but when you cease working with the agency you either have to pay them to hand over the account or start again from scratch. It can also mean that if you part company with the agency that ran your PPC, you no longer have access to the data collected during that campaign, such as which ads/key phrases were performing best, and thus you will need to start the test and learn process from scratch.

- A final consideration: **how much work you are getting for your budget**. Many PPC campaigns are managed for a monthly fee, but when the campaign is up and running successfully it is very easy to sit back and just let things tick over without doing any work. For this reason, instead of a monthly bill that just reads 'Campaign Management', you need a breakdown of what work has actually been done. The Google Adwords system can track all changes made to a campaign over any given period, which can help you get to the bottom of what work has been done. Even when getting these work breakdowns, look out for the catch-all 'Keyword Research'. It is a valid activity, but you need to understand what keyword research was done and what the output was.

SEO and PPC working together

We need to consider how SEO and PPC can work together effectively as part of our digital branding. I am often asked whether you should bother with PPC advertising if you are already ranking number one for a search term in the organic search results. The only way to truly get an answer to that question is by testing it. Look at your results with and without PPC running and you answer the question precisely. This testing is even more necessary with mobile search, because of the different user focus and motivations. You will certainly get some cannibalization – that is, people clicking on your paid ads who would have clicked on your organic search results, but you need to understand what additional traffic you can get and then look at how PPC and SEO traffic convert differently.

Search conclusions

Search is an effective and essential part of your digital marketing toolkit and will make up an essential part of the user journey. Therefore, it has a huge impact on our digital branding. Making sure we fully understand our target audience, their motivations and requirements, and mapping this to the content we provide (and optimize), is a fundamental requirement for any organization. This means that effectively planned and implemented search campaigns can be one of our most important business drivers and can have a huge impact on our digital branding.

Mobile   07

The main problem with the concept of mobile marketing is that it immediately makes us focus on the device. In reality, this is actually one of the last things we should be thinking about. To put this in context we can try to answer a couple of questions. How big does my phone have to be before it is a tablet? How about if the screen on my laptop flips over and is a touch screen, is it then a tablet?

The reality is that the line between mobile and non-mobile devices is blurring and will continue to do so as technology changes (we already have a device that is somewhere between a mobile and a tablet that is being referred to as a 'phablet'. (This is by far one of my least favourite new words to come out of the mobile world!) What this tells us is that mobile marketing is not all about the device; it is about the changing user journey. As I have said repeatedly, we need to focus on and understand the user journey in order to maximize our digital branding efforts. What it means is that our digital branding needs to take into account the changes to the user journey caused by mobile devices.

This alignment with the user journey and what the consumer actually wants is essential and, although it sounds obvious, is more often than not completely missed in mobile marketing campaigns. The reason that this basic concept of alignment with consumer requirements is missed is that we (or the partners and agencies we work with) are blinded by the technology and creative options.

Technology for the sake of technology

Just because we can build an app doesn't mean we should (in fact, you really need to think about mobile sites before apps in the majority of cases, but more on that later). Using technology inappropriately without setting objectives or having a clear business case is nothing new.

From my experience, the majority of business Instagram and Facebook accounts are set up with little or no idea as to why it is being done. It happens because someone senior has decided it is a good idea without understanding it, someone junior did it without asking anyone, or someone in the business has seen that competitors are doing it and so feels that an opportunity is being missed. It doesn't mean that it is necessarily the wrong channel or a bad idea, but anything done without objectives or a business case is generally doomed to failure.

AI everywhere

Some of the most impactful changes with the world of mobile recently are the advances in artificial intelligence (AI) and the fact we can now have AI assistants built into the apps we use every day. Since the launch of ChatGPT version 4o, the speed at which AI voice assistants were able to respond went below the 1 second mark, making them far more useful and conversational than before. This increase in speed, and therefore the reduction in friction felt by the user, has led to a rapid advance in the use of AI within apps and the mobile device operating systems. The ability to search with an image or video, to translate text in real time using augmented reality (more on this later) and to identify an animal by the sound of its call, are all features in every day apps now (in this case the Google App and MerlinID). Those brands that don't adopt the opportunities that AI offers, will soon find their user experience is clunky in comparison to their competitors.

User journey and context

I have mentioned the user journey a few times already, but let's try to understand this in a bit more detail. We need to understand what our target audience might want to achieve, understand their path to doing this, see how mobile fits in and then provide the right experiences and content to achieve these objectives.

Some of this will be the *discovery phase* (also referred to as 'push', 'stimulus' and in a dozen other ways!) where we are trying to build awareness, educate and stimulate some form of further action. Some will be in the *engagement phase*. These are activities that are driving engagement, experiences and moving towards the user's final objectives (see Table 7.1).

The line between discovery and engagement becomes increasingly blurred as we move into location-based interaction (engaging with a brand when in-store, for example), but these phases can start to lay a foundation for us

Table 7.1 Discovery and engagement phases in mobile marketing

Discovery phase	Engagement phase
Mobile email	Mobile sites
Mobile display ads	Apps
Mobile paid search	Mobile optimized social media
Mobile organic search	Mobile payment and couponing
Offline stimulus (QR codes, etc)	Location-based interaction (near field communication, etc)
Push notifications	

when thinking about where mobile fits into the user journey. However, this is currently a fairly one-dimensional model that only really talks about mobile marketing techniques, while acknowledging that things like offline marketing may exist.

Local intent

I have so far left out mentioning the local-based consumer. Not because this type of consumer is not important but because it can be a distraction from the broader picture. If your business has any sort of location-based offering it can be immensely powerful, but this goes back to our concept of understanding the target audience's objectives and context, and then using mobile technologies to deliver the most appropriate solution.

According to Smart Insights, 92 per cent of smartphone users have their phone by their side day and night (Chaffey, 2024). If I am looking for a local hotel, my nearest bus stop, a nearby provider of power supplies for my brand of laptop and so on, this type of search is transformational to the mobile user and any potential business involved.

Integrated devices

Our expectations of mobile device are radically different now and smartphones and tablets offer us fully integrated computing and telecommunications devices.

This integration is what has led to the radical change in usage that we need to understand in order to make best use of mobile marketing.

When we consider the level of internet searches done on mobile devices, social media interactions, and email reading and writing (all of which we will explore in a moment), we quickly see that what we are doing with the device becomes far more important.

The technology distraction

It is easy to get bogged down in working out which mobile devices your app should work on, what happens when a new phone version comes out and how effective your responsive design website is. All of this stuff matters because of the final outcome of your mobile campaigns, but the reality is that your mobile consumers don't care. They just want to be able to get stuff done.

Responsive design means absolutely nothing to the majority of the people on this planet and nor should it (and maybe to you right now, so we'll talk about this more in a moment). You need to worry about the technical aspects of your mobile strategy but your users shouldn't. They shouldn't even notice it.

Mobile compatible is not mobile optimized

Just because your website works on mobile devices does not mean it is mobile optimized. What I mean is that the site may load up fine on my phone, but if I have to zoom in a dozen times to see anything clearly, this isn't an optimal experience.

What we need to consider now is what my target audience is likely to do, in what context and on what devices. I can then start to make sure I have ticked the appropriate boxes to make their experience as pain free as possible.

With regard to the amount of time it takes for a site to load, users are even more impatient on mobile devices than they are when using a desktop or laptop (Hewitt, 2017). They have come across so many poor mobile sites that they just give up very quickly. On the other hand, if we can create a seamless mobile experience we stand a better chance of achieving our objectives and can actually build loyalty.

Technology challenges

So, you are thinking something along the lines of: 'It's all very good saying the technology doesn't matter, but I have to make choices and every time I make a change it costs money.' You are 100 per cent right. The reality is that this has always been the case in marketing. We have to decide where to spend our money and how to prioritize our budgets. The actual problem here is that the number of options is large and we don't ask the right questions.

Asking the right questions

Rather than asking whether you should build an Android or iOS app (if you have no idea what I'm talking about, take a look at the box below), you should actually be asking what devices your target audience use and which groups it will be most cost-effective to reach. Let's frame this for a moment by forgetting about mobile. If I decide I am targeting an audience, but I can only afford to target 50 per cent of it, I need to decide which 50 per cent. I don't do this based on an opinion; I most likely do it based on the potential lifetime value of that customer, how much it will cost to target them and other commercially focused criteria. The same applies to the different mobile platforms and choices we make within our mobile strategies.

PLATFORM WARS

It is worth understanding the key players in the mobile operating system (OS) market. For the sake of simplicity we've just looked at the major smartphone and tablet platforms here. An OS is just the software that a phone runs on and will impact its functionality and, most importantly for us, apps built for one platform generally don't work on another. The key players are:

- **Android**: Google's mobile OS. It is open source, meaning it can theoretically be used and adapted by anyone. It has also been adopted by the Open Handset Alliance (OHA), which includes big handset manufacturers such as Samsung, Sony and HTC.
- **iOS**: Apple's OS used on its iPhone, iPod, Apple TV and iPad product range. It is closely associated with OS X used on Apple Mac computers.

> Beyond these platforms with the largest market share there are a whole lot more. Take a look at Wikipedia to see just how many (and then don't worry about them! By the way, if you are going to send me hate mail about telling people to ignore your particular mobile OS of choice, you should probably get out more): http://wikipedia.org/wiki/Mobile_operating_system.

Audience segmentation

Just because 40 per cent of the world uses a particular type of mobile OS, it doesn't mean that your target audience in your target market does. For this reason you shouldn't rely on a lot of the generalized statistics that are published. If you do need some initial guidance, take a look at the next chapter, which tries to summarize the key trends and statistics from each region of the world.

In reality, your target audience probably won't align with the norms of your particular market, and if you are working across multiple regions it clearly gets more complicated. What we really need to do is to collect some actual market insights, as we should with any other aspect of our marketing. You can do this by sample surveying your target audience and actually asking the question as to which type of mobile OS they use.

Frictionless technology

What we are aiming for is to make the process of achieving the consumer's goal as simple and as transparent as possible. This idea of making the process as seamless as possible is often referred to as 'frictionless technology'. What we should always consider in our mobile marketing is what the objective of the user is, and how that can most effectively be achieved using the right technology in the right place.

Mobile sites and responsive design

Let's make something clear from the outset: you need a mobile optimized site. That doesn't mean that your site happens to work on mobile devices: it means the user journey via mobile has been carefully considered and you offer the optimal experience via mobile devices. It means that you have weighed up the different technical solutions in order to achieve this and have selected the most appropriate approach. It also means that you have not been steered by the limitations of your current web platform or content management system (CMS).

Start with the fundamentals

As of 2016, the majority of website visits were on mobile devices (Titcomb, 2016). In 2021, Google moved to mobile-first indexing (Donnelly, 2021), meaning that they read the mobile version of your website to decide what it was all about. Putting mobile first is key to delivering effective digital branding.

Focus on the user journey

The key point of a mobile optimized site is to offer an experience that best suits the consumer's needs and setting. This means they should be able to access the information or utility that your site offers, on the device they are using, in an easy and efficient way.

Responsive design

Responsive design, sometimes referred to as adaptive design (although these definitions actually mean different things, as explained below), means developing one site that will display differently on different devices. This means that the site can look completely different on different devices and will layout in a way best suited to a particular device.

This approach is generally implemented using a combination of web technologies. The key point is that these technologies allow the browser to look at things such as the device that the site visitor is using, the width and height of the display, and then decide on how the page should be laid out (see Figure 7.1).

Figure 7.1 A great example of responsive design in practice, showing the Target Internet website (http://www.targetinternet.com) – Figure 7.1a as the full-width version, and Figure 7.1b, the same site with the browser width reduced

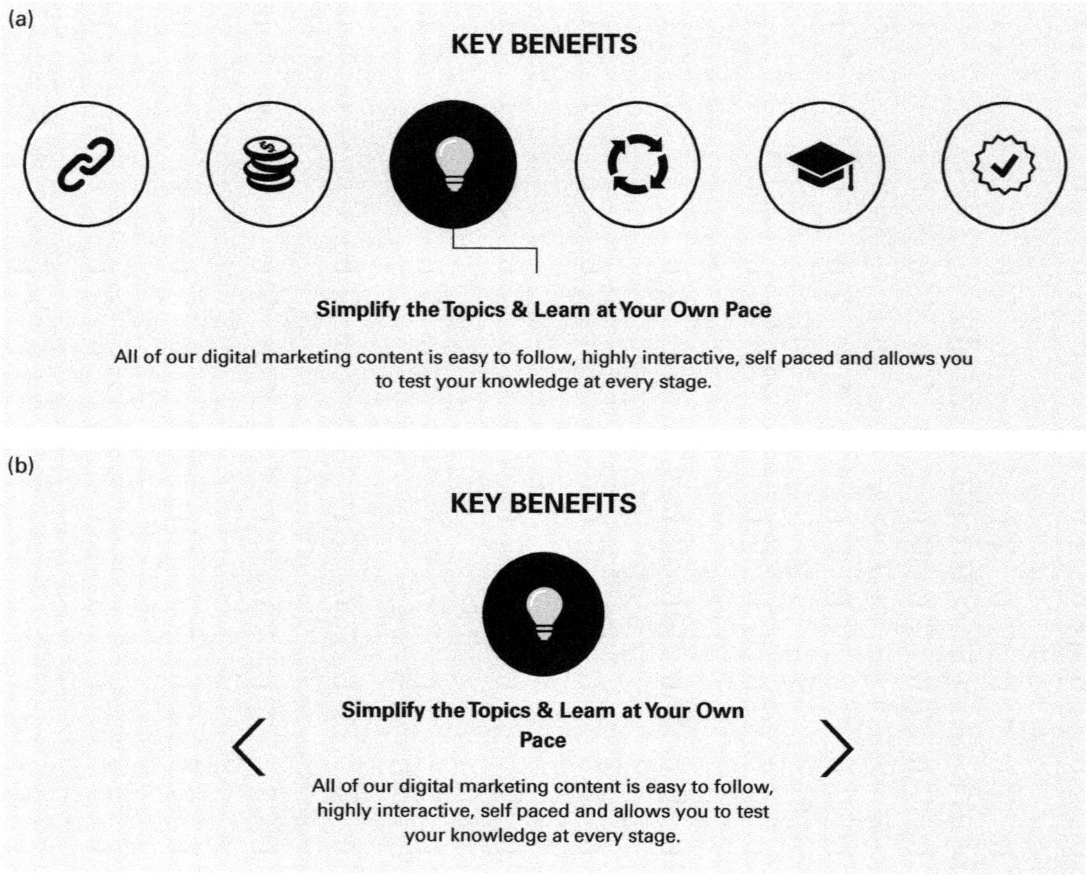

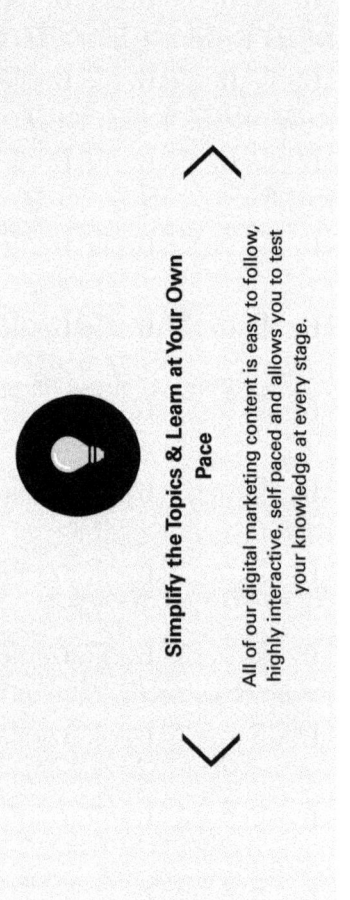

> **RESPONSIVE VERSUS ADAPTIVE**
>
> Responsive design and adaptive design are often terms that are used interchangeably, yet they are quite distinct.
>
> Responsive design is something that is actioned within your browser. This means that a page is sent to your browser and your browser then does the work to display the correct elements of the page. This is called a 'client side' technology (the client is your browser).
>
> Adaptive design is something that is actioned on the web server. The type of device being used is discovered and then the appropriate version of the site is delivered. This is called a 'server side' technology.
>
> The advantage of adaptive design is that not as much content is sent to your browser, where it may not be used, and a solely mobile version of a site is sent to a mobile device.
>
> The term 'responsive design' is gradually coming to mean adaptive design, although developers will argue about the differences for evermore.

Mobile apps

Many organizations rushed out and built apps just because they could. I witnessed dozens of conversations that started with the words 'We need an app' and ended in protracted discussion about what it could do, and how much it would cost. As we discussed in Chapter 5 on social media, however, just because you can do something doesn't mean that you should.

Mobile sites first

If you don't have a mobile optimized website, forget about getting an app built and get the mobile optimized website fixed first. We have already talked about the huge increase in traffic to sites on mobile devices, and the reality is that this is more likely than an app to be a user's initial experience of your mobile presence. It's not that apps aren't also important, but in reality you most likely also need a mobile optimized site.

Bolstering value proposition

Just like any marketing activity we need to start by aligning our business objectives with user requirements and decide how our app can help achieve this. One thing that apps can be fantastic at is bolstering value proposition by delivering some form of online utility or entertainment.

Mobile conclusions

Mobile is not about the device; it's about a changing user journey. For our digital branding to be effective we need to embrace these changes and the potential added complexity that this presents. It means that the technology behind our websites needs to adapt quickly to the changing devices that our audience will be using, but this needs to be seamless to their experience.

Online advertising   08

Let's start by being cynical (or perhaps realistically pragmatic!). Online advertising is probably the easiest aspect of digital marketing to waste your budget on and carry out ineffective campaigns. This is because banner ads are the easiest part of our digital branding to understand from a traditional advertising perspective. This means that many traditional marketers' approach to digital has been to create print/TV ads and then create digital equivalents of these in a banner format. This approach is generally poorly targeted and not adjusted accordingly for the digital channel it is delivered through. Much of the blame for this lies with agencies that don't really understand digital but also because it is a channel that lends itself to a 'broadcast' approach. I have said that justifying marketing activity for which we could calculate the return is often put down to 'brand building', and this has been particularly true of banner ads. As click-through rates go down, we persuade ourselves that it is not about the click, but we do little to measure its effectiveness. We will remedy that in Part Three, but in this chapter we look briefly at the key factors involved in online advertising and how they impact our digital branding.

The positive side of online advertising is that we now have a wide range of creative and targeting options that can improve the effectiveness of our ads, along with the analytics and metrics to judge their success. I am not against online advertising, but it is always wise to keep your eye on the end objective.

Online advertising is fundamentally about various forms of banner advertising, including video ads and, as mentioned in Chapter 6, paid search is a form of advertising. In fact, due to the amount of different creative options, the term 'banner advertising' doesn't really cover all of the different things we can do with digital ads.

Advertising objectives

Just like any other aspect of digital branding we should start by clearly defining what our actual end objectives are and how online advertising is going to contribute to these goals. The reason this is even more important to define when considering online ads is because of the way they are often priced and measured.

Much online advertising is still sold on a cost per mille (CPM) basis. This basically means that you pay a certain fee every time your ad is shown 1,000 times. This means that you are paying for display, not even clicks, and certainly not for results. This isn't the only option, but it is the most common. The result is that it is very easy to waste budget on views of your ad that are seen by completely the wrong audience.

Your ad being shown once is called an 'impression'. If I hit refresh 10 times on a page with an ad on it, that will be 10 ad impressions. Also, if a page loads that my ad is on, but the ad is below the fold (below the part of the page that I can see without scrolling down), and the user doesn't scroll down the page, the ad will still have had an impression even though no one saw it. The impression also doesn't tell you how long the user was actually on the page that the ad was shown on. This page view duration is referred to as 'dwell-time', and even if my dwell-time was half a second, if the ad loaded, an impression gets counted. We clearly need to look carefully at what we are paying for.

Another challenge with online advertising is that results are often measured on a click-through rate (CTR) basis. The reality, though, is that even if we get clicks it doesn't mean that the visitor who drives to your site will necessarily carry out the action that you want them to. They may leave your site as soon as they arrive. Equally, someone who doesn't click on your ads may interact with them in some way and go on to make a purchase. This means that we need to find better ways than CTR to measure the success of an ad.

App advertising

As well as the options for advertising on mobile sites, we also need to consider ads within apps. This may be from the perspective of running ad campaigns in appropriate apps that are used by your target audience, but it may be from the perspective of making money by placing ads within your apps.

On both iOS and Android you can integrate ads from a wide variety of different ad networks (more on this later). All of these solutions generally work by automatically placing ads within your apps (in the locations you have developed into the app) and then giving you a share of the revenue made from the ads.

If you want to advertise within apps, then there are a number of different ad networks you could go to (again, more on this later) or you could approach an app owner directly to negotiate a deal.

Ad networks versus media owners

An ad network manages the advertising space on a number of different locations that may include both websites and apps. They offer a range of targeting options and then place your ads within the sites/apps they manage according to your targeting criteria. Different ad networks have different targeting criteria, which can vary from fairly basic options such as category matching (automotive, finance, etc) all the way through to things such as behavioural targeting.

Generally, ad networks charge a fee and then share some of this with the owner of the location that the ads are shown in. They provide the technology for placing the ads, the account management to the advertisers and provide some form of reporting for all parties involved.

Ad networks are why there are standard sizes and types of ads. This means you can create an ad once and it can be run across multiple properties (mobile sites and apps) without the need to redesign every time.

INTERNET ADVERTISING BUREAU

The Internet Advertising Bureau (IAB) is the trade association for online and mobile advertising. It promotes growth and best practice for advertisers, agencies and media owners. The IAB has sites for regions around the world sharing best practice and define the standards for sizes and types of ads. This includes the various types of mobile ads, and defines things such as how big they should be in regard to screen size, file size, etc.

The global website can be found at **http://www.iab.com/** and they also have local market sites, which are listed on the main website.

Rather than going to an ad network, you could go directly to a media owner. A media owner is someone who owns a site or app (or even email list) that you may wish to advertise on. Going directly to a media owner has the advantage of knowing exactly where and how your ads will be shown (this often isn't true when using ad networks because some ad placement is 'blind placement', meaning you set the targeting criteria but don't get to choose the exact sites that your ads are show on). The disadvantage is that very often you are targeting one site or app at a time and they don't have the targeting technologies available via the ad networks. They may also be limited in the types of creative options they offer and the reporting facilities they provide.

Targeting options

Different ad networks offer different types of ad targeting, and I have summarized the most common of these below. One network normally doesn't offer all of the options, and different networks will have access to place advertising on different websites. Thus you may need to work with multiple ad networks to achieve your campaign objectives. The most common types of targeting are:

- **Location:** place your ads based on location-based criteria such as country, city and distance from a physical location. This option can also be used to exclude as well as include an area.
- **Demographic:** target by criteria such as age and gender. This may be based on users having registered their details or it may be based on some sort of modelling basis, in which case it is worth understanding how these data are modelled and how likely the data are to be accurate.
- **Category:** one of the simplest forms of targeting, based on the category of the content within the site or app. For example, automotive, finance, etc.
- **Content matched:** the content of the page the ad is being placed on is read and ads are matched based on content. This is how ads are placed within Google's display network. This can be effective, but just because I am reading a news story about pirates doesn't mean I want to buy a boat!
- **Behavioural:** there are lots of different approaches to behavioural targeting, but generally these rely on being able to see a user's behaviour across a website (or number of websites) and then targeting ads accordingly. I may be looking at an automotive website, but if I have just been on three websites looking at credit card deals, then it is perfectly valid to show me an ad for a credit card on the automotive website.

- **Re-targeting**: this allows you to show ads to users who have visited your site before. So, for example, if I visit your site but don't buy anything, I could then be shown ads for your site on other websites.

Creative options

This is where things start to get very interesting. The amount of different creative options for display ads is exploding. A few of the more common options are listed below, along with a pointer to where to find some great resources for getting creative inspiration (a black and white book doesn't really do interactive online advertising full justice!):

- **Banners**: images can be displayed with or without animation, and users can tap the banner to be taken to a variety of destinations.
- **Expandable**: expands an ad to cover the full screen upon a tap, without removing the user from the app or mobile browser experience.
- **Interstitial**: displays full-screen rich media ads either at app or mobile browser launch or in-between content pages.
- **Video**: various options to place video before/after/during other video content or within other rich media formats.
- **Mobile**: there is a wide range of video based and interactive mobile ad formats, but be careful, many are intrusive CTR and can be misleading as users click by accident.

Ad reporting and analytics

Most ad networks will provide reporting tools, but ideally we should integrate our advertising data with our mobile and app analytics so that we can get an integrated view of our mobile marketing efforts.

An initial step is to make sure that all of our mobile ads are tagged with analytics tracking code. This allows us to identify any traffic coming from our mobile ads to our sites and apps and then track this through to conversion. Instructions on how to do this for Google Analytics are outlined in Chapter 14.

Taking things a stage further, in Google Analytics 4, Google now allows you to export data from Google Analytics using BigQuery and you can combine this with ad network data for even greater insights.

> **GOOGLE ANALYTICS AND SINGLE CUSTOMER VIEW**
>
> Google realizes the importance of having all of our sources of data from digital marketing in one place so that we can effectively manipulate and analyse the data to make smarter marketing decisions. GA4 (the latest version of Google Analytics) allows you to export data using BigQuery, and Google Data Studio allows you to bring data from a wide range of data sources into one place to build interactive visualization.
>
> https://www.google.com/analytics/data-studio/

Online advertising conclusions

The display advertising market is currently highly fragmented with a wide range of ad targeting, features and creative options. Just like any form of advertising, the results of campaigns are highly variable based on the options used and the overall effectiveness of approach. For this reason, any online advertising efforts should be carefully considered and tied back to business objectives, with a clear methodology put in place from the outset for tracking and measuring results.

The varied, and often highly interactive, creative options available are very impressive. However, if we go back to our initial concerns about user objectives, we need to ask some very searching questions before making assumptions about the effectiveness of any online advertising campaigns.

It is very easy to be sold online advertising on the basis of its 'brand impact'. Don't forget it is one of many touchpoints and, as the easiest to understand from a traditional advertising and branding point of view, it is often over-relied on. Map out the user journey, work out where it fits in and then measure for success.

> **VIEWPOINTS**
> Ciaran Rogers, Host, The Digital Marketing Podcast
>
> **Are your brand campaigns hooked on junk data and lies?**
>
> I recently came across a great little story that struck a real chord for me when I think of online brand campaign management. The story is of two

friends who leave a pub. As they leave a little the worse for wear, Bill trips on the steps as he leaves the pub. Initially carried along with the crowd, his friend Steve notices his drinking buddy has dropped back and goes to find out what the problem is. Bill is on all fours under a streetlamp across the road from the pub's entrance.

'What are you doing?' Steve asks.

'I'm looking for my contact lens, it fell out when I tripped on the step leaving the pub,' replies Bill, scouring the street floor.

'But the steps for the pub are the other side of the street!' laughs Steve.

'I know that Steve, but the light is much better here under the lamp. I won't find anything over there in the dark!'

A bit of a daft story, until you realize that in many ways, brand analytics measurement solutions, which drive such important spend and campaign allocation decisions, can be equally absurd. We end up looking where the analytics light shines a light, and more often than not it shines light on easy-to-measure last-click channels. I don't blame the tools. They can do a lot more if you push them but default last click is where we all feel comfy; happily scrabbling around in the light looking for the answers with Bill. But what if the answers are on the other side of the street?

I'm happy to place a bet that brand advertising on AdWords will be some of your most successful campaigns in terms of cost and ROI. But what is fuelling that activity? Do we really believe consumers blindly stumble into entering our brand names into search because you are such a shining beacon of brilliance? Or are we a little more realistic and realize that rising star of your PPC campaign is being fuelled by much harder-to-measure multiple touchpoints both online and offline?

Where are the sweet spots you need to do more of? Your online display? The radio ads you ran? The TV slots you funded at huge expense last quarter or the (delete as appropriate) in-store activity / email campaigns / word of mouth / blogger outreach / the amazing stream of brilliant content marketing you work so hard on / social media campaigns / social sharing by fans / trade show leads / direct mail campaign / number one organic listing for popular niche keyword combination / YouTube video content you did at the start of the season?

Face facts and realize you need data to guide you here. Don't rely on opinions from within your organization. In my experience they are massively influenced by the campaign elements individual team members or agency teams have a part in delivering. We all see what we want to see sometimes!

Any one of your campaigns could be working fantastically well and fuelling your fabulously easy-to-measure last-click channel success, but your analytics won't tell you because real customer journeys en masse don't all flow from one click. They never have and they never will.

To make matters worse, mobile devices, which now make up over 50 per cent of traffic for a lot of organizations, are shifting the way analytics records direct-to-website traffic. Since 2016, mobile browsers have been effectively bookmarking any web pages their device owners have visited, meaning you only need to type the brand name into the address bar of your mobile browser and the helpful smartphone will magically transport you to that location and leave the data-hungry digital marketer with a handy note in analytics that you just showed up without any campaigns or mediums influencing or directing you to your end goal. Not at all helpful when you want to allocate marketing spend to the online channels that are driving results.

Making matters even worse, most consumers are consuming your online content via multiple devices and also in some cases via multiple browsers. Cookie tracking that analytics solutions use struggle with this. Each cookie being stored is typically measuring visits from one particular device and worse still stores it in a browser-specific folder. As a result, cross-device browsing behaviours make a mess of your analytics customer journey and attribution measurements. But the problems don't stop there. If you think your online measurement is a challenge, how then do you start to attribute success to any joint online–offline real-world consumer hopping? We know it goes on. We all do it, but brand managers tend to conveniently ignore it because it's just too difficult to get our troubled little egos around.

As a result, PPC, email and affiliate activity are the most addictive part of the online brand direct response world these days. They are great at measuring close-to-conversion online activity, which you can capture with some simple URL tracking codes but not so great at anything you can't add Analytics UTM (tracking code that we add to our campaigns to help tracking in Google Analytics) tracking URL values to… simply set them up and start counting those large conversion attribution values that roll into the reports. Everybody loves big numbers, right?

Solutions

So what is a brand hooked on the buzz of last-click attribution supposed to do? Well the first step to recovery is always recognizing you have a problem! Like many addictions, denial is the hardest of all the issues to overcome, but once you have admitted you have issues, your search for solutions can take you in a number of directions.

Take a good long hard look at all of your top-of-funnel campaigns that help your brand name and awareness grow. Look at the costs of these and take a serious look at how you are going to measure and attribute this cost to the results it drives. If your budgets allow, invest some time researching and investigating a good data management platform, which will provide you with smarter segments for smarter targeting and personalization of your campaigns together with much smarter attribution. If budgets don't allow for this, then you are going to need to take third-party cookie data into account for your display campaigns. Most display campaign solutions will require tracking code to be set up and this can give you valuable insights into what the broader online brand activity is achieving. Remember, people don't tend to click on display campaigns, but those exposed to reminders of your brand definitely show an increased likelihood to consider you and purchase from you in most tests I have run. But don't take my word for it. Set up the tracking and test it out on segments from your CRM and see what difference those exposed to the campaigns show compared to those who are excluded from the campaigns. For consumer brands, Facebook advertising and tracking solutions offer a great place to start with this kind of smart segmentation and attribution, but don't stop there. Run some tests and if you get results, broaden your campaign reach with other platforms and solutions.

It's only when you get brave and start to play around and turn off some of the funding for these last-click channels that you begin to realize that actually your brilliant campaign/campaigns are not the revenue-driving power houses you thought they were. Don't believe me? Try it. Start turning off some of this easy-to-get paid activity and see if you still get the business. Be selective and take things a step at a time. How many new customers are each of these channels bringing home to roost? If you can get it, that information alone can give you a lot of confidence with where to experiment for improvements and efficiency.

What about the pure brand PPC campaign your PPC agency is so fond of? How much of the mobile device traffic to that campaign was mobile users clicking on the first link that showed up under their click-happy thumbs? Thumbs that would very happily have landed on the number one organic listing you most likely get for those pure brand terms had your PPC campaigns held fire and given them the chance? Feeling a bit braver? Did that affiliate promotion really drive the results it claimed or do you get the business anyway because most of it was from customers who have just learned to find affiliate links to get a discount on stuff they were going to buy anyway? Try turning it off for a week or two and see if your top line revenue drops as much as the affiliate tracking claims it makes. I'd be very surprised if it does. And while you do this… check out the savings you make. All of this is valuable fuel that could be given to effective channel activity, fuelling your brand's progress and success.

Use last click to measure what it's good at. For top-of-funnel activity take a look at first click or get familiar with more sophisticated analytics attribution models like time decay or, better still, a custom attribution model. The free version of Google Analytics allows you to compare different models to better understand how channels all play tag together, so take it for a spin. You might also be able to make use of third-party cookie data from your display advertising solution and include this separately when reporting on your results. Speak to your display campaign partners to find out how they can help you with campaign attribution for your marketing channels.

Offline retailers should really focus on offering email receipts. Armed with this you can marry up more of your online and offline activities, which can be a real help. What can you do to ensure you get these? In most cases you just need your retail teams to ask. It's a real benefit to the consumer to have a receipt that's way harder to lose. Try asking them!

With a few probing questions, and a few data-driven brave steps, there are a lot of gains and improvements you can accomplish, and with each step you will feel bolder, stronger, and more in control of your activities and brand. I won't lie, it's a tough path to tread but then so are all worthwhile paths in life. Here's to luck and good fortune on your journey.

Email marketing   09

Around 40 per cent of emails are now opened on a mobile device (MailButler, 2024). The reality, however, is somewhat more complicated. Many of us use our mobile devices to 'triage' our emails, that is, we use our mobile devices to monitor our incoming email and respond to anything urgent. Non-urgent and more complex email is generally responded to from a desktop or laptop in many cases (this is a reflection of the limitations of mobile devices in many cases still). This means we need to make sure our emails are fully optimized for the multiscreen journey to give the optimal brand experience.

Focusing on the user

In this chapter we will look at each element of email marketing in turn, but we need to keep our target audience at the heart of this journey. Bear in mind your ability to target, personalize and maximize the impact of your emails will be highly impacted by your email service provider (ESP). For example, in Figure 9.1, you can see the options in Hubspot (a popular ESP and customer relationship management (CRM) that we will explore later in this chapter) for previewing your emails on various mobile devices to make sure the user is having the optimum experience.

Email isn't exciting

I don't agree with this statement one bit, and I'll explain why in a moment, but let's start with an example. If I run a webinar or a conference talk and I include the phrase 'latest trends in social media', I am pretty sure I'll fill the room (virtual or otherwise). However, if we talk about some element of email marketing, it just won't get the same level of response. Most of us are interested in what's new and what's changing, and many of the core principles of email marketing have been the same for some time. The issue is that

Figure 9.1 Using an ESP (Hubspot) to preview email display on various devices

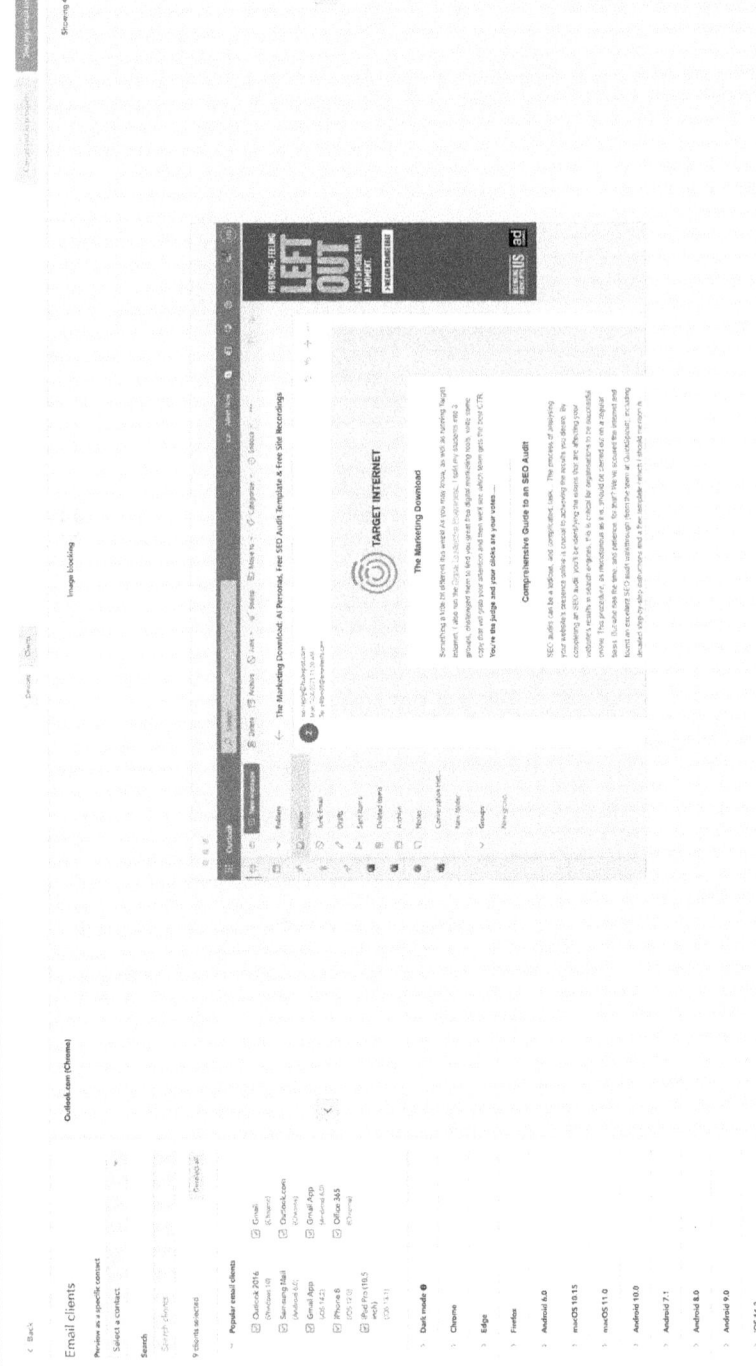

not many of us are following these principles and we would rather try something new than improving what we are already doing.

Ease of iteration

The single greatest thing about email, in my opinion, is the ability to test, learn and change quickly and easily. Trying different versions of pages on your website or creating different apps can be expensive, time-consuming and often fraught with technical problems. Trying different email subject lines, calls to action and length of copy are all extremely easy to test assuming you are using the right ESP.

An ESP will allow you to store email lists, create and send email campaigns and track results for you, and how well suited your ESP is to your needs will have a direct impact on how effective your email campaigns can be. There are dozens of different ESPs out there, ranging from the basic, through to highly sophisticated systems that could be used as CRM systems in their own right. We will explore what we need from an ESP in more detail in a moment, but first we need to look at the state of the email market and dispel some myths.

AI tools and email

Generative artificial intelligence (AI) tools like ChatGPT and Gemini can be extremely helpful when planning and building email campaigns. Most email platforms allow for easy A/B testing of subject lines and content, that is, testing one version of an email versus another to see which is most successful. Generative AI tools make it very easy to come up with multiple versions of a subject line, copy or call to action that can then easily be tested (Figure 9.2).

The training data that these generative AIs are based on, includes thousands of previous emails and their results. Therefore these tools can also do a pretty good job of predicting which versions of a subject line may be most effective before we've even sent a test email.

As with all content, we can use these tools to assist with content creation, but it must be with the intent of creating great content, not just pumping out more content.

Figure 9.2 Email AI ChatGPT suggesting five alternative subject lines

> suggest 5 subject lines for an email targeted at digital marketers with the latest digital marketing news

1. "Stay Ahead: Top Digital Marketing Trends You Can't Miss"
2. "Breaking News: Latest Digital Marketing Insights & Strategies"
3. "Essential Updates: What's New in Digital Marketing This Week"
4. "Unlock Success: Must-Know Digital Marketing News & Tips"
5. "Fresh Off the Press: Cutting-Edge Digital Marketing Developments"

THE DECLINE OF SPAM AND RISE OF BACN

You are probably very aware of the concept of spam, defined as unsolicited email communications. As we have said, spam is actually on the decrease and a range of security and technology solutions are helping to progress this fight. What is generally on the rise, though, is BACN (pronounced bacon). BACN is defined as the range of emails that we have signed up for but don't see as relevant and never read. Over time we subscribe to more and more newsletters, we get service and social media updates we never read and are generally getting more email that, although not truly spam, is not relevant or useful to us.

Increasingly, webmail clients like Gmail are trying to separate this kind of email from emails that are relevant by placing these emails under separate tabs. Different systems have different ways of judging the relevance of an email, but very often it is based on user behaviour. If you regularly open and click on email from a particular address, these systems will learn your behaviour and identify that an email is relevant and they are more likely to place this email in your main inbox. Therefore, getting engagement and clicks on every one of your emails becomes even more important as it will impact whether your future emails are seen.

There also services like **Sanebox.com** that offer us services to help filter our email, unsubscribe from unwanted newsletters and summarize lower priority content. All of this means that if our emails are not seen to provide value, our target audiences just will not see them in the first place.

Focusing on relevance

This movement towards separating essential emails from promotional emails means that if we use email as a broadcast channel, focusing sales messages, we are likely to get lower and lower response rates. The nature of mobile users trying to 'triage' their email means we have precious few seconds to demonstrate the value of our content. We need to focus on using a range of techniques and technologies available to us to make our email as tailored, relevant and useful as possible to our audience, and that's what we'll explore in this chapter.

This doesn't mean that you can't send promotional emails with products and special offers. If I ask you to send me special offers that is what you should do, but they need to be the right offers for me, sent at the right time at the right level of frequency. And if I've signed up for a newsletter, don't just send me sales messages. The general approach I apply to email marketing when not working on an e-commerce basis, and an immediate online sale is not the proposed outcome, is to consider the principles of content marketing. There should be a ratio of commercial and non-commercial content in your emails, and by that I mean really providing value through your email content. Many of my clients work on an 80/20 rule – that is, 80 per cent non-commercial useful content and 20 per cent about stuff they want to sell you. I would suggest you go even further and aim for a 90/10 or 100 per cent non-commercial content. Providing useful content is the single best way to get your email known and remembered, increase the likelihood of future email opens and to drive traffic to your site. Once you have the site visitor, you have the opportunity to build trust, awareness and potentially drive someone along your sales funnel.

Email and the user journey

Once we understand the impact email marketing has on our potential user journey, and how effectively it can work as one of our digital touchpoints, we can start to really look at the great ROI email marketing can offer.

> **THE IMPORTANCE OF TRACKING CODE**
>
> When we look at our web analytics to try to understand where our web traffic is coming from and how it is impacting our bottom line, our traffic sources are an essential report. In Google Analytics these are found under the Acquisition reports and this is broken down into some key areas. Organic search is traffic from sites such as Google (but not paid advertising from these sites), referrals are visits from other websites, social are visits from social websites and then we come to direct visits. Supposedly direct traffic is traffic that comes to your site when somebody types your web address directly into their browser or has bookmarked your site and visits by selecting that bookmark. What direct traffic actually represents is visits that your analytics package has no idea where they have come from.
>
> This is a really important thing to understand in regard to email, because unless we add tracking code (which we'll explain in a moment and cover in more detail in Chapter 14) to the links in our emails, then people clicking on these links will show up as direct traffic and we won't be able to differentiate where they came from. So when we send out our email campaigns, we will see an increase in direct traffic, but we won't be able to identify that 100 per cent as being a result of our email.
>
> Tracking code basically involves adding some information to each of our links, so that when a visitor arrives on our site we can use our analytics to identify exactly where they have come from. You can see the Google URL Builder that allows us to generate this code in Figure 9.3. It is also possible that your ESP gives the option to automatically add tracking code, which can be a great time saver.

Going beyond last click

To understand how email is having an impact on our overall marketing efforts, we need to understand where it fits into the user journey and how it is impacting the bottom line. We may expect somebody to read our email then directly buy our product or fill in our lead generation form. However, it is more likely that email will be one of many touchpoints that build up our relationship over time.

For this reason we need to consider the analytics results from our email campaigns carefully and make sure we are going beyond the last click. We

Email marketing

Figure 9.3 Using Google URL Builder to generate tracking code for an email campaign

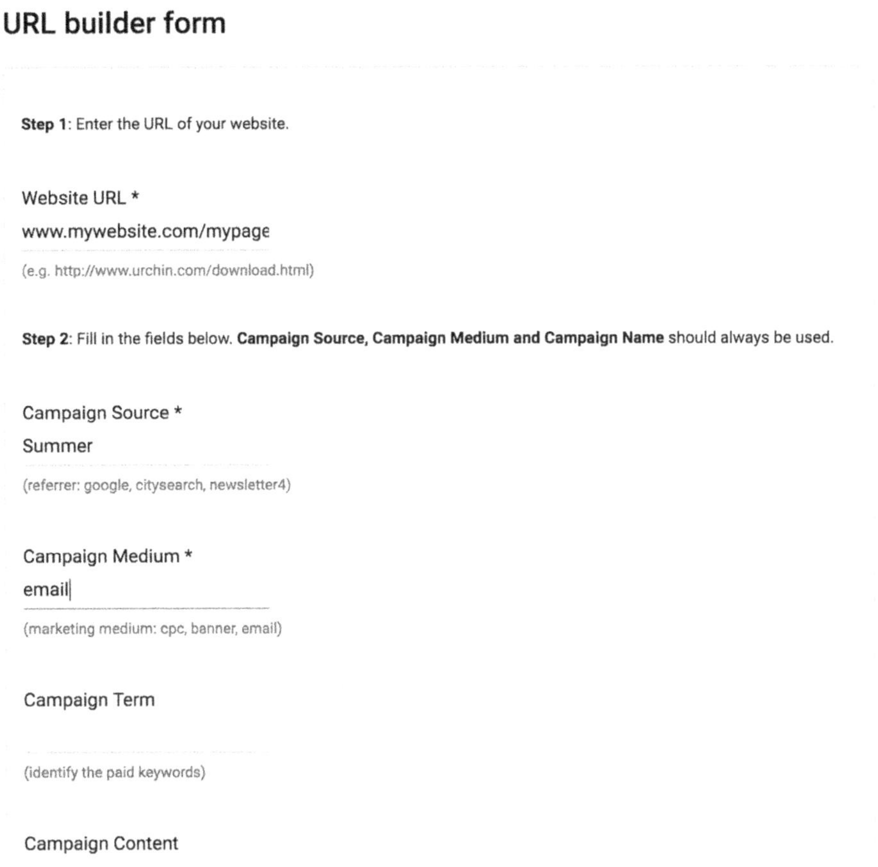

URL builder form

Step 1: Enter the URL of your website.

Website URL *

www.mywebsite.com/mypage

(e.g. http://www.urchin.com/download.html)

Step 2: Fill in the fields below. **Campaign Source, Campaign Medium and Campaign Name** should always be used.

Campaign Source *

Summer

(referrer: google, citysearch, newsletter4)

Campaign Medium *

email

(marketing medium: cpc, banner, email)

Campaign Term

(identify the paid keywords)

Campaign Content

(Google and the Google logo are registered trademarks of Google Inc, used with permission)

Figure 9.4 Considering each step in the user journey and going beyond a 'last click' mentality

explore this idea a lot more in Chapter 14, but at this point it is necessary to understand each step of the journey that leads someone to carry out an action that we desire. For example, as we can see in Figure 9.4, there may be a number of different paths through to conversion. As we can see at the top of Figure 9.4, I may get an email, sometime later do a search resulting from something I experienced in that email and then go on to carry out some form of online conversion. Alternatively, as we can see at the bottom of Figure 9.4, I might have just done a search and immediately converted. In both cases, if we looked at analytics from a 'last click' perspective, in both cases the source of the conversion would be seen as the search, as this was the last click before conversion. By that logic, we might challenge why we are even bothering with email marketing and pull the plug on this activity. But if we do that, we won't get the search that followed and we won't get the conversion.

So in order to really get the most from analytics when we are thinking about email marketing, we need to have tracking code in place and make sure we are looking beyond the last click. Happily, Google Analytics provides some excellent reports to allow us to do this in the shape of 'multi-channel funnels'. We look at this report in more detail in Chapter 14, but essentially it allows to us see what channels a visitor to our site used up to 90 days before they convert. That is, what are the different steps and channels that were used in any of the user journeys that ended with one of our goals being completed.

Selecting an email service provider

To really get the most out of email marketing we have said we need to focus on relevance. In order to do that we are going to need to think about segmenting our data, targeting the content, testing different elements of our campaigns and really making best use of the channel. To do that, and to make it easy to do, we need to select the right tool, and generally that will be some form of ESP. These tools generally work around three key areas: building, segmenting and targeting your email list, building and sending your emails and, finally, giving you reporting on the results. Each of these areas can be extended to offer all sorts of functionality such as scheduling, automatic triggering and social media integration, all of which we will explore more of later.

The key thing is, you don't want to get stuck with a system that limits your capability, but you also don't want to pay for things that you don't need. We've highlighted a few different ESPs in this chapter, but there are new entrants all the time and many are very similar. To help you choose, some of the key considerations are listed below.

> **ENTER THE MONKEY**
>
> MailChimp is a very popular and very low cost ESP. It has a very intuitive interface, loads of advanced functionality and is one of the cheapest ESPs on the market. It is also fully geared-up to help you build mobile-optimized campaigns. They charge by the size of your list, rather than by how many emails you send, which can be a real cost saver if you are sending a lot of emails.
>
> So what are the downsides? First of all, all support is done online, meaning you don't have an account manager you can call on. Also, it is a self-service system, and although the interface is very straightforward, it is down to you (although there is nothing stopping you from bringing in a third party to assist you). You also need to pay using a credit/debit card, meaning if you can't pay this way, it is not for you. Also, if you need some form of customization or really advanced integration it may not be the right choice (although they do have an API that lets developers do all sorts of things with the system).
>
> I love MailChimp: I use it for some of my businesses and I love the fact that it means I can test and learn quickly and easily. There are lots of other ESPs out there, but MailChimp is often a very good starting point: **http://www.mailchimp.com**.

Gaining opt-ins and building a list

In order to do any email marketing we are going to need to collect an email list, and the rules on how we can collect data change from country to country. It is also not just a matter of following the rules, but really about following best practice in order to assure the quality of our lists and avoid annoying our target audience. Like many things in digital marketing, we tend to get distracted by volume when carrying out email campaigns, and the question often asked after each campaign is 'How many emails have we sent?' and 'How many people are on our lists?'. What we should really be focusing on is the quality of our lists and the actual results achieved by our campaigns. We actively don't want people on our list who don't want to receive our emails, otherwise we are just creating a negative touchpoint that will damage our brand image. I am sure you can think of at least one company that keeps emailing you with irrelevant or overly sales-based content, and over time it creates a negative impression of that brand.

Best practice in regard to opt-in is to follow a 'double opt-in' approach. That is, to allow somebody to fill in a sign-up form (more on that in a moment) and then send them an email that they need to click on in order to confirm their opt-in. This might sound like a slightly laborious process but most ESPs will fully automate this process for you. Also, the fact that the user has filled in a form and bothered to click on a link achieves two things: first, they have self-qualified by showing they are actively interested in what you have offered based on the fact that they have actually made some effort to sign up; second, this sign-up process gives you actual evidence they have signed up, otherwise anybody could take your email address and sign you up for any email list!

Sign-up forms

Rather than trying to collect huge amounts of data at the point of sign-up, which will be a barrier to getting opt-ins, I generally recommend you keep the amount of information you ask for initially to a minimum. You then have the opportunity to prove the value of your emails and ask for more information by using surveys, questionnaires or polls on an ongoing basis. You also need to consider the types of data you may want to collect, think about whether you will really use these data and whether your ESP is capable of storing it and using it. We may also want to think about how we are going to move these data between our ESP and our CRM, but this is a topic we will cover in detail in Chapter 10.

MOBILE AND SIGN-UP FORMS

One of the greatest and ongoing frustrations for mobile users is pop-over email sign-up forms. For example, you visit a website and are reading a great blog post. After a few seconds a pop-over form covers the page and asks you to sign up to the website's email list. This is no problem on a laptop: you simply click the close window button on the top right corner of the pop-over. Unfortunately, many of these pop-overs are not built with mobile users in mind, and the close button is unreachable on a mobile device, leaving the user stranded on a useless page. If you are going to use pop-over forms, it is essential to thoroughly test them on mobile devices.

The two key things that concern people when they are signing up to email lists are what you are going to do with their data and how often you are going to email them. Ideally, at this stage you will clarify both points with a statement along the lines of 'We will never pass on your details to a third party, and we won't email you more than once a week'. You can also have a link through to your privacy policy that outlines clearly what you do with data, but in my experience very few people read these.

List segmentation

As you build an email list, you need to consider what differentiates the individuals on your list and what kinds of different content may be relevant to each of these segments. It is essential that your ESP allows you to collect data and add fields of information to your list in a way that will be practically useful for segmenting your lists in the future.

For example, you may want to send different emails to people living in different geographical locations and you will therefore need to collect and store these data. It could be that you want to store these data separately in your CRM system, and we will discuss these options in Chapter 10, but for now let's assume we are adding more information to our ESP list.

Different ESPs have different approaches and limitations to this, but increasingly many ESPs allow you to add a huge number of additional fields (in some cases an unlimited amount) that you can then use to segment and personalize your email.

> **THE BENEFITS AND RISKS OF PERSONALIZATION**
>
> Personalization in emails generally refers to the process of inserting personalized content such as your name, job role, company name or location into an email. It can also refer to the process of segmentation or dynamically building content, but we will explore these concepts later.
>
> So if we are talking about inserting your name into an email to personalize it, what impact does that have? Different studies show different results, and it certainly has to be seen in the context of your overall email efforts, but there is generally a small increase in CTR. However, if you get the data wrong and insert the wrong job title or name, the damage will far outweigh any good you would have done. Therefore, only do this form of personalization if you trust the quality of your data 100 per cent.

We can segment our lists in a number of different ways but we are generally talking about segmenting our lists based on collected data and by preference. That basically means that we have collected some information from an individual on our list and then used this to personalize their email. This may be in the form of sending particular content, sending a particular format of email or sending at a particular time or frequency, all based on what data you have collected.

This approach can be very effective in making emails more relevant and improving open rates and CTR. In fact, improvements of around 15 per cent in open rates and up to 63 per cent in CTR are entirely possible when taking this approach (MailChimp, 2017).

Open rates and click-through rates

Two of the most commonly discussed statistics we get from our email campaigns are open rates and click-through rates. It is worth understanding these in a bit more detail so that we understand where they are useful and what their limitations are.

Open rate tries to tell you how many people have opened your email. I say tries because, unfortunately, owing to the way it is calculated, it is inherently inaccurate. An email is registered as open when an image in that email has been loaded. So, you bring up an email in your email client, one of the images loads and that tells the ESP that the email must have been opened.

This image is generally a single pixel image hidden at the bottom of your email, often referred to as a web beacon. There are two problems with this approach. The first is that even if you open an email for half a second and then delete it, as long as the image loads, the email will show as being opened. Although this is technically true, the open rate doesn't really paint a true picture of what happened. The other problem with relying on images being loaded to indicate an email being opened is that when an email is viewed on an email client that doesn't load the images, you won't know it has been opened. It has been suggested that around 50 per cent of users don't see images automatically, which could mean some fairly unreliable data being reported as open rates.

This doesn't mean we should abandon looking at open rates, however. In fact, we are still using them as a benchmark – as at least we are comparing like for like from one campaign to the next or within split testing (discussed below). We just can't rely on them as an entirely accurate representation of how many people open our emails.

Click-through rate (CTR) is the other key measure we to tend to look at and, although a far more accurate measure, we can rely on it too much. Obviously, getting a click on your email and driving a visit through to your website is great; however, that is just part of the journey. It is entirely possible that everyone who clicks gets through to your website, takes one look, doesn't like the look of it and leaves immediately. You could, therefore, have a campaign with a 100 per cent CTR that was a complete failure!

So CTR is a useful measure but we then need to look at the visitors' behaviour on our site to really understand the true impact of our email campaigns. For true commercial insights we will need email reporting, web analytics and for goals to be set up in analytics. We will also need to understand how these goals impact our business outcomes (and that is what Part Three of this book is all about).

This does highlight one of the potential weaknesses of email marketing, however, and that is even if you have the best email campaigns in the world, if your website doesn't match that standard, your campaign won't be as effective as it could be.

Email design

We could fill an entire book with discussions about email design best practice, what works and what doesn't. The reason for this level of discussion is that the effectiveness of the design will depend on your target audience, the email client and device the email is being read on, and a host of other factors. What that means is that we need to test for our particular list and, in fact, we may find that different designs are more or less suitable for different lists and even segments of our lists. We will explore all the different things you can test for your particular list in the testing section of this chapter, but the key principles that every email should take into account are highlighted here:

- **Minimum font size:** Apple recommends 17–22 pixels (px) and Google recommends 18–22 px for mobile devices, so go for a minimum of 18 px.
- **Header images above the fold:** don't place large header images at the top of emails. They push your content further down the page, and when images are switched off your audience won't see anything apart from a missing image.
- **Blocked images display:** consider what your email will look like when images are switched off. Make sure you have a 'click to view online' link (most ESPs will add these automatically). Also, make sure all of your images have alt text as this will display in place of the image in many email clients when images are switched off.
- **Call to action placement and size:** consider where on the page your call to action will appear in various email clients and try to keep it visible above the fold (before a user needs to scroll down to see the content). Bear in mind the bottom right, where many calls to action end up, may not be the most suitable place and you may need multiple calls to action. For call to action buttons, Apple recommends 44 px squared and Google recommends 48 px squared for mobile users, so go for the higher of the two, 48 px.
- **Scannability:** users try to assess the relevance of an email as soon as they open it and decide if it is worth reading properly or not. Make sure your email is scannable and that the key message comes across clearly and easily. Avoid large blocks of text, complicated layouts and poorly defined calls to action. Don't have multiple links close together.
- **Unsubscribe:** every email should have an unsubscribe link in the footer, and this will generally be automatically inserted by your ESP.
- **Footer:** the footer of your email should also include your physical postal address if you wish to be compliant with US email regulations (CAN-SPAM).

> **RESPONSIVE EMAIL DESIGN**
>
> Responsively designed emails attempt to adapt the email according to the device you are displaying it on and the size of display that screen has. This means that an email will display differently on a smartphone, a tablet and a laptop screen. However, just as there are limitations in what we can do with email design versus web design, there are limitations to the effectiveness of responsive email design.
>
> This limitation is because most responsive design principles rely on the support of media queries, a technique used to understand the size of a screen and then adapt things accordingly. Unfortunately, media queries are not supported by all email apps. At the time of writing the most noticeable of these are the Gmail apps for iPhone and Android phones (although this may change soon).
>
> For a great summary of which apps do and don't support media queries take a look at the excellent guide on the Litmus website: **https://help.litmus.com/article/206-which-clients-support-media-queries**.

Email templates

You have a few options to consider when creating emails and the templates that you use. You can design your own templates from scratch, edit an existing template from your ESP or use a template from another source. Each of your emails could be different, but in terms of brand consistency it makes sense to modify a particular template for a particular style of email each time you send one. So, for example, you may have a newsletter template, an e-commerce template, etc.

Most ESPs will provide a set of standard email templates that you can modify for your own use and many also provide a visual editor that lets you edit these templates without any coding skills. Alternatively, you may need to edit your template code yourself and upload the HTML. You could do this editing yourself if you have the skills or use a designer/developer to do this for you. Many ESPs offer these kinds of service at an additional cost or you could use a freelancer website like UpWork.com. Always remember though, email template design is a very specific skill, and just because somebody can design a website, it doesn't mean they know all the peculiarities of design for the wide range of email clients.

The digital toolkit

Figure 9.5 Litmus.com allows you to preview what your email will look like on a wide range of clients and devices

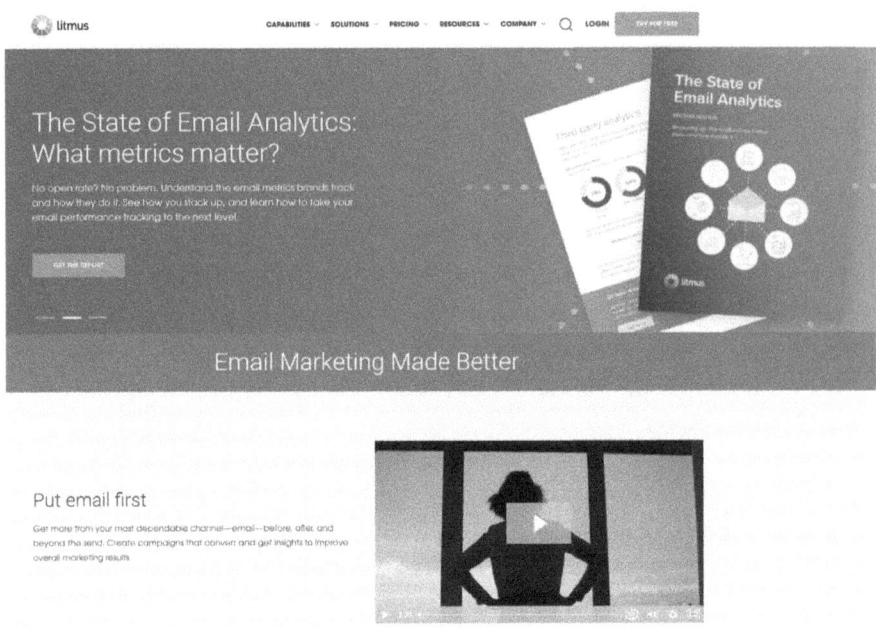

The most important thing to do with your email template is to make sure it displays properly on different email clients and devices, and to do this you have two options, one easy and one hard! The hard option is to manually test your email template on every possible different email client and device combination. This very quickly becomes an impractical task because of the number of possible options. This is why inbox inspectors were created, in order to simulate what your email will look like on each of these different display possibilities. Many ESPs have these built in, but if your system doesn't you can use a system like Litmus, shown in Figure 9.5.

SPAM CHECKING

We have already discussed the improvements in technology that are leading to the increased detection of spam emails. Unfortunately, the side effect of this is that your email could be mistaken for spam by the many spam filters in operation and never reach its intended destination. In order to minimize the chances of this happening you can use a spam filter testing tool. This will try to gauge the likelihood of your email ending up in a spam filter and will point out the key things you may want to change in your email.

Your ESP should have one of these tools built in, but if it doesn't, Litmus.com also offers this service.

Sending and testing

Once you have created your great email content and built the perfect targeted list, you will want to send your emails. There are quite a few things to consider at this stage and a range of testing options is available to you.

Many ESPs will allow you to carry out A/B split testing very easily, or you can manually split up your list in order to this. The basic principle is that you take two segments of your lists and send each a variation of your email, testing a particular feature of the email (this could be subject line, copy length, etc). You then learn from these tests, work out which one got the best results and can apply this learning to the remainder of your list. For example, you could take two segments of your list, each consisting of 15 per cent of the total list and run a test (making up 30 per cent of your list overall). You then learn from this list and send out the better variation to the remaining 70 per cent of your list.

Open rate or click-through rate

When carrying out these tests, depending on what element of our email we are testing, we will need to look to the open rate or the CTR for our results to judge which is the most successful. We can split these two measures as follows:

Open rate: subject line, send time, from address.

CTR: all variations within the email content.

Once we decide what element of our email we are going to test, we also need to decide how long we are going to wait after sending the initial two tests until we judge the most successful and send to the rest of our list. You can see how easy some ESPs make this process in Figure 9.6.

Figure 9.6 The easy-to-use interface for sending A/B split test campaigns using MailChimp.com

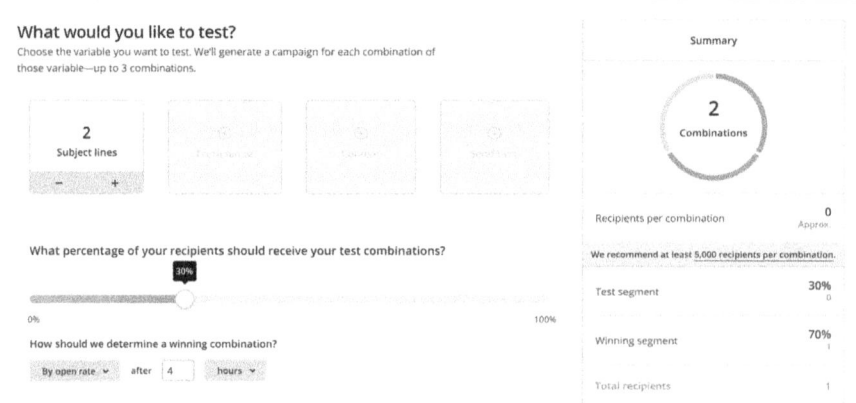

Something you do need to consider, however, is how the period of time you wait after sending your initial emails before you send to the remainder of your lists will impact your results. If you send out the test segments on a Tuesday and then send out to the remainder of your list on a Wednesday, you will potentially skew your results, because people react differently to emails on different days of the week.

You could wait a clear seven days and send your follow-up email at the same time of day and day of the week as your test email, but even then you may find that things have changed over a week due to the time-sensitive nature of your news story or similar.

There is actually no 100 per cent ideal solution to this problem, but what you should do is understand which days of the week work best for you and how different days of the week compare. You can then choose to send your test and follow-up email on days of the week when your audience reacts in similar ways.

Dynamic content generation and rules

So far, we have talked about building a list, potentially segmenting this list and then sending out content, with various testing opportunities. Many ESPs allow you to take your email marketing a stage further and generate even more well-segmented and personalized emails. They do this by not only looking at preference data, that is data that have been collected from the individual, but also by collecting behavioural data dynamically and generating emails based on this.

This could be as simple as a triggering an email a month since the last email click-through. It could, however, be a lot more complex and look at behaviour on your website and use this in order to adjust what content is sent out in an email. If an individual looks at a particular product, why not send them an email about that product? If they put an item in their basket and didn't buy it, why not send a follow-up email? Based on what they have clicked on in the last five emails, why not customize the content in the next email based on these interests? Different ESPs allow you to do different things, so it is worth considering from the outset the kind of dynamic personalization you may want to carry out. Some ESPs take this even further by thoroughly integrating with CRM systems and we could even then start to look at the topic of marketing automation. We will look at these two topics in more detail in Chapter 10.

MESSAGE BANKS AND BUSINESS LOGIC

An increasingly common approach to solve the problem of sending too many emails on various different topics to the same individual is to use a message bank system. The basic concept is that we send a single email that contains a number of different stories or pieces of content, but these pieces are selected and prioritized dynamically for a particular individual, based on a set of rules we define.

The rules we define can be simple or complex, but they dynamically select content and place it into a particular order from a 'bank' of messages (hence the name). This is only possible in some ESPs and there are some key challenges to consider. If the rules are too complex, we may need too many pieces of content in the bank to meet all of the requirements we have set. It is also possible that some parts of our list never receive a particular type of content because other pieces are always prioritized over it. The key here is to build your rules carefully, not get too complicated and test all of the possible outcomes.

Email marketing conclusions

Email marketing is a hugely flexible area of digital marketing that can be an extremely effective part of our digital branding. It is also something that can be done badly very easily, so a suitable level of planning and resourcing is essential to get it right. Selecting the right ESP will impact everything you do in your email marketing efforts, so select carefully and then make sure you are making full use of the various targeting and testing opportunities available.

In a privacy-focused web, could email save your brand?

In 2021, the digital privacy tide began to turn rapidly, and with every ebb and flow, it favoured individual users, not marketing. After years of marketing and advertising abuse, user privacy became important. The signs a privacy storm was brewing had been there for many years. Even before 2021 dawned, GDPR legislation in Europe and the California Consumer Privacy Act (CCPA) in the US started a snowball of new privacy regulations in multiple states and countries designed to curb the marketing privacy invasion. As consumers and customers, we all know how easy it has been to harvest our data and use it to stalk us as users wherever we go in the digital world.

The Cambridge Analytica scandal brought the excesses of digital privacy violations into sharp focus. As a result, privacy regulation became ever more rigorous. Prominent players in the digital world began to take pre-emptive steps to stem the flow of personal digital information. Apple led the charge with changes to how their Safari web browser blocked third-party cookies and removed first-party cookies after a set period. As a result, programmatic advertising/customer stalking became much harder. Web browser providers embraced a privacy-first approach for their users. Even Google, one of the largest ad serving networks on the planet, announced that 2021 would see their Chrome browser blocking third-party cookies, and they started doing this in 2024.

IOS email shake up

Apple's IOS update in April 2021 further shook things up. Suddenly, tracking through apps wasn't the secret marketing source it once had been.

Facebook woke up to the realization that they didn't directly own a significant portion of their audience. With their April 2021 IOS update Apple insisted their app store users grant permission to any app looking to track users behaviour. As most IOS users use the Facebook App to access Facebook, almost overnight, large portions of Facebook's online community could opt out of Facebook's behavioural tracking ecosystem. It created a real storm of concern among the social media advertising community. Large portions of the Facebook audience suddenly couldn't be tracked as they had been. Behavioural targeting for those users couldn't be recorded, quantified and sold to advertisers.

Apple's move to ask app users to opt into such behavioural tracking made social media stalking by brands much harder. You can't blame Apple. They gave users a meaningful choice. Users overwhelmingly embraced the option to retain their privacy. It turns out consumers don't like marketers and advertisers doing things to them. They want control. They want a choice. Who knew?! The rapid adoption of ad blocking software and *en masse* adoption of Apple's privacy choice sent a very clear message. The digital stalking party was over, and with it, a vast swath of the digital landscape needed to operate via new rules.

Against such a backdrop, your brand and your audience's relationship with that brand have never been so important. At the heart of it, that relationship is the key that will unlock digital access to future digital audiences. The privacy-focused digital environment is here to stay, and brands needed to adjust their approach to recruiting and retaining large audiences.

Against this backdrop of a brave new user privacy-focused web, email marketing has become the most potent permission-based channel at every brand's disposal.

For many years, the number of global email users almost precisely tracks the estimated number of internet users. Why? Because you get given access to email by every internet service provider. The two go hand in hand. Every office-based or work-at-home-based job in the developed world comes with an email account. It's almost omnipresent. Like electricity, it's part of the essential mix. Every major social media channel leverages email to keep users engaged and coming back for more. Why? Because the engagement architects that design better and better engagement know we regularly check in with that channel. It's the fastest and most cost-effective way to reach a global audience at scale. We are all of us at the email party via one email account or another.

An Adobe study in 2019 found that the average white-collar worker spends around five hours a day on email each weekday! In case you were wondering, on average, that broke down into three hours of work email and two or more hours on personal email. No social media platform in 2021 could boast such impressive engagement stats.

Email should be adopted as a core channel by any brand serious about engaging with their brand audience at a deeper level.

CAN-SPAM Act

Email has been a permission-based channel for many years. The US CAN-SPAM Act started the legislative ball rolling in 2003, demanding double opt-in mechanisms for regular list email subscribers. In 2016, GDPR legislation in the EU further strengthened email's permission-based credentials by requiring that users freely opt in to receive ongoing email messaging. It demanded that it must be as easy to give this permission as it was to revoke it. The penalties for ignoring these demands were extreme. The marketing world took note and somewhat reluctantly adjusted its practices.

Email as a social channel

So is email a social channel? Well, that depends on how your brand chooses to operate. There is no shortage of brand email campaigns that still run on a batch and blast one-list, no-user-preferences basis. If you are one of those brands, listen up. Email now marches to a very different tune, and it isn't of your brand's making. Your subscribers set this tune and beat. It's policed by powerful AI algorithms that take no prisoners. Fail to play by the new rules, and your email efforts will achieve nothing.

The social channel you own

Unlike mainstream social channels, your brand owns the relationship it has with email subscribers. In the digital world, we increasingly see that ownership of relationships is crucial. Third-party cookie tracking across multiple websites is being shut down and blocked by adblocking software. Social media properties can and do get shut down as well. Remember Myspace? Remember Google My Business? All the work and investment put into those properties when they were riding high fell by the wayside when they fell from grace.

Changes to how mainstream social channels function can hit your marketing reach hard. At Target Internet, we built a large community of podcast listeners on a LinkedIn group. Following GDPR legislation, LinkedIn changed how group owners could communicate with community members. Suddenly our LinkedIn group became useless as a communication platform. It was frustrating, but there was nothing to be done.

When these changes happen, you realize you don't have control. You don't own the communities you build on social media like you own the relationship with email subscribers. The social media party always starts with lots of free organic reach and engagement, but eventually, commercial pressures come to pass, and the free reach dries up, and you are forced to pay to play. That doesn't happen with email. Social media platforms own and control access to their community of users. They are third-party communities. We have learned that third parties can be pretty brutal when allowing brands access to their users. Email is much more first party. It's your channel, your party, and your subscribers individually choose whether to stay and indulge in that party or grab their coats and move on to a better venue.

The rise to power of the inbox providers

With email inbox providers facing ever-growing waves of unsolicited emails, the need to act quickly and work smart has become a top priority. However, staying ahead of marketers is hard enough when they're just harvesting addresses; throw AI into the mix that can send billions at scale, and it becomes an uphill battle for those trying to stay afloat in this sea of spam.

If all of the emails sent got delivered, the medium would have been considered broken years ago. You wouldn't be able to see the messages that matter for all the junk.

Legislation demanding unsubscribe links has helped, but the AI inbox providers have set up the real breakthrough. It monitors user behaviour to determine what is essential and what isn't. Email users no longer just have an inbox. There's the 'other stuff that's been sent to you that isn't as important' box. What ends up in that other stuff box is the content we don't race to open, never reply to or repeatedly ignore if it does get into our inbox. Brand email marketers reap what they sow. Send dull, repetitive or irrelevant messages, and at scale, and you can kill off your brand's email visibility. User behaviour controls who gets to see what. It's a genius user-focused move, and it works pretty well most of the time.

Ever since the beginning of social media, online platforms have been using user behaviour to decide who gets to see more of what content. The fundamental difference between social media algorithms and email inbox algorithms is that no one organization owns email. So it's way more democratic a medium. Social media algorithms pay close attention to what users want, but they also tend to favour brands prepared to pay for broader exposure.

The secret to online engagement

The alarming truth is that you can get a lot more attention in today's digital world if you give your audience stuff they want. Create useful or entertaining content time after time and watch the engagement grow. Keep on broadcasting dull brand-related propaganda, and users will switch off and disengage.

But it isn't enough to just get your emails opened. You need to get your email users to engage with the content. Personalization helps stack the odds of this happening in your favour, as does regularly cleansing your list of users who have stopped engaging. Large email lists in 2024 are a liability. It would help if you had higher percentages of engagement. Fail to achieve this, and the inbox user behaviour algorithms will file your message into 'Other stuff' quicker than you can say 'double opt-in mechanism'.

Designed for engagement

And on the subject of double opt-in mechanisms… you are using them, aren't you? You should be. Not only because it's a legal requirement of the US CAN-SPAM Act and helps prove you got permission for GDPR purposes. There is a much stronger reason for adopting it in our opinion. Double opt-in helps establish trust. Trust from your brand that the user exists and wants to engage. Trust from the user that your brand only wants to send them stuff they want. And most importantly… trust from the inbox provider that emails from your brand got opened and clicked on from the very first send. So double opt-in processes help to improve ongoing visibility and engagement.

Up your game

Stop employing out-of-date practices that you think save you time and money. They can damage the flow of positive engagement signals to the inbox providers.

Are you still using DoNotReply@ or NoReply@ email addresses to send your brand's emails?

'Don't speak to me. I'm too important.'

Brands need to find more welcoming ways to retain the respect and loyalty of their email audiences. For example, you wouldn't throw a party and refuse to allow guests to speak to the host. That isn't polite. Don't make the same insulting mistake with those at your email party.

Why on earth would you not want an email subscriber to reach out to you and engage with your brand by asking a question or even placing an order? That kind of behaviour should have died out with the Dotcom boom/bust era. You wouldn't dream of ignoring users on mainstream social channels, so why downgrade your email subscribers to second-class partygoers. Every engagement from your audience is an opportunity to be better. Every question is an opportunity to understand and improve. Embrace two-way communication. It's the key to better inbox placement for those who love your brand.

And the learning and engagement doesn't stop there. Like any good community manager, you need to obsess about what your users like and give them more of it. Don't just think regular mass sends. Go beyond this. Create opportunities from the knowledge of your customers you gather in your CRM system. Focus on each customer's interests, previous purchases and problems. Be a force for good in every customer's life. Other channels can help you, of course, but email gives you direct contact at scale every time.

Embracing the change

Email marketers just need to get more creative with how they approach positive customer signals via email. Ask questions, create mini questionnaires or engaging experiences your customers can't resist. The engagement you get will be way more meaningful and insightful than an email open. More creative brands have already moved beyond the simple email open as a signal the message worked and got read. Instead, why not build in a simple thumbs up or smiley feedback mechanism. Use that to gauge how recipients felt about the email. You won't get as much data as you might feel you got from the open rate, but you will quickly learn across many emails when you have a winner.

I hope the arguments and discussion in this chapter have inspired you to be more social with your brand's approach to email. It's the most incredible channel in my experience working for many brands. It feels like it's been around forever and in digital terms, it has. However, I still think that we haven't even really started to scratch the surface of what's possible with email. And as the privacy-focused winds of change ravage the effectiveness of other channels like programmatic display and social advertising, the savvy marketer is focused on not just sending emails. The smart money in marketing knows the real long-term value of building meaningful relationships between the customer and a powerful, much-loved brand. So don't focus on building your list. Instead, build on the strength of your customer/brand relationship. No one can take that relationship from you if you stay true to your customers' wants, hopes, needs and desires. It belongs to you and your customers. The future success of your marketing may well be built upon its firm and sturdy foundations.

CRM and marketing automation

10

We looked at email marketing in the previous chapter and explored the great opportunities it offers in terms of personalization and the positive impact this can have on your digital branding. This can be taken a step further by integrating your email service provider (ESP) with your customer relationship management (CRM) system, and there are even more opportunities when we explore the possibilities offered by marketing automation systems. We begin this chapter by exploring CRM systems and their relationship with email and digital branding overall, then move on to the practicalities of automation systems.

Definitions and practicalities

Customer relationship management

CRM systems are basically where you store your customer data. As well as basic information such as contact details, the idea is that you store the history of your engagement with your customer, what marketing you have sent to them, any responses and so on. The systems are also not limited to customers and can be used to store information on potential leads, partners and suppliers. There is a wide range of suppliers of CRM systems and the breadth of what they can do is constantly growing and changing.

What you are aiming to do with CRM in regard to digital branding is to personalize any marketing you carry out so that each touchpoint is adapted and well suited to the needs of whoever you are talking to.

If you know what I have bought from you previously, my geographical location and various other things about me, you are able to make smarter marketing decisions. This means you can be more relevant and this enhances each touchpoint you have with your audience, thus improving your digital branding.

There are differences and similarities between CRM systems and what ESPs offer, but very often there is some blurring of functionality between the two things.

Marketing automation

Marketing automation is the process of not only triggering automated communications but doing this triggering according to a scoring system. This scoring system is what differentiates marketing automation from advanced ESPs, because many ESPs can do various forms of triggered communications already (such as sending an email based on a user's website behaviour). Automation scoring allows us to set rules and thresholds based on both behaviour and information we have stored about someone. So, for example, I could decide to trigger a particular email to you, based on what pages of my website you have looked at, how recently you looked at them, the fact that you attended a webinar last month, the size of your company and your job title.

Marketing automation is generally best suited to help with the sales process of complicated products where the buying cycle takes weeks, months or even years. This means it is generally applied to B2B products and services, although there is no reason why it cannot be used for more complicated consumer products such as cars.

Single customer view and bringing data together

One of the things that is required in order to use ESPs, CRM and automation systems effectively is the integration of these systems and the information they contain. The idea behind this integration is that of 'single customer view', which basically means that all of the information I have about you is accessible in one place so that I can make smart decisions.

Figure 10.1 shows the ideal scenario where we bring together all of our different systems so that we can use this information to make smart decisions. So, for example, I can send you the right information by email based on your previous email clicks, what you have done on my website and what you have said in social media.

Figure 10.1 The 'single customer view' achieved by bringing all of our sources of information together

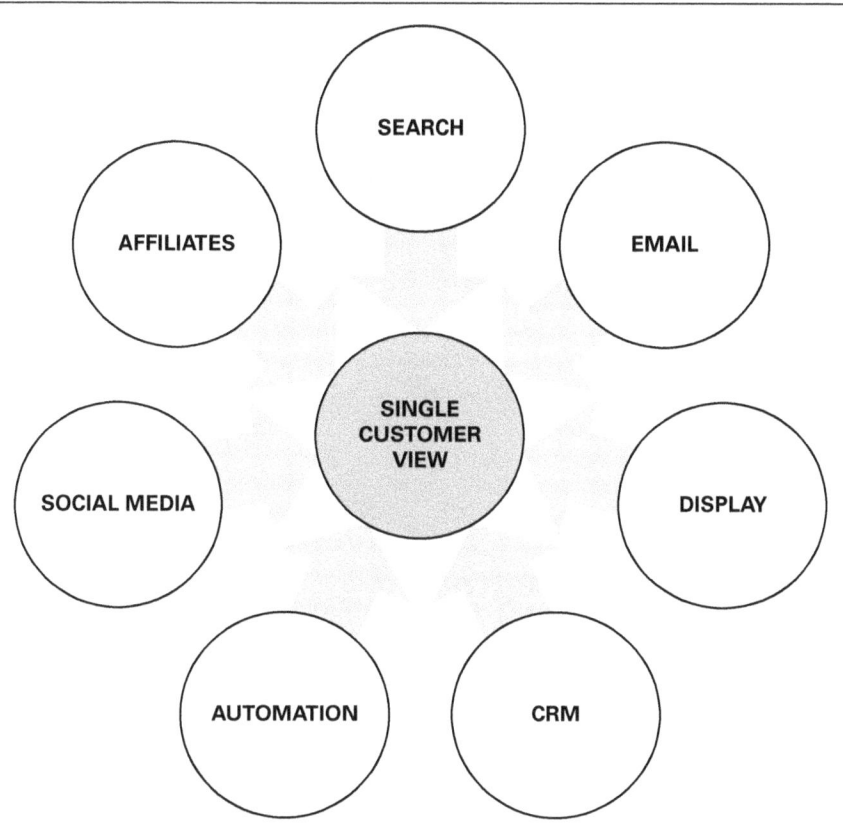

Essential and very difficult

The concept of a single customer view sounds like a great idea, and it is, but unfortunately achieving it is generally not easy. The reason for this is that what we are basically talking about is an IT project, and if there is one type of project that generally goes over budget and over schedule, it is an IT project. You may be wondering why trying to achieve single customer view has got anything to do with IT, and it is basically because we are trying to bring together systems and databases. If you are a small organization with little in the way of existing systems, or you are starting from scratch, this isn't a great problem. However, if you already have existing systems, you may find they are not compatible and need customization – and the whole thing is a headache. My general advice on this, though, is that you should persevere, because I honestly believe that achieving this integrated view is what will differentiate between business success and failure for many organizations in the future. Let's explore why I believe that this is the case.

Smart marketing and agility

The environment we operate in is changing very quickly. Business and marketing continue to evolve at a dramatic rate, and our potential customers are all living in this environment. This has huge implications for our organization's need to test, learn and adapt quickly. Integrating our systems to achieve a single customer view means we can interrogate the data we have and hopefully use it to make smarter marketing and business decisions. This is hugely important from a digital branding point of view, because a company that is slow to react and continues to broadcast messages, rather than personalize and have a two-way dialogue, will damage their reputation and erode customer trust.

CRM and ESP integration

In many cases it is perfectly possible to send emails directly from your CRM, without the need for an ESP. There are, however, a number of downsides to this approach and I would generally avoid it (although if you are using an online CRM such as Hubspot, these have excellent built in ESPs).

The key downsides to using your CRM to send emails are around spam filtering and potential blacklisting. When you send from your CRM, you are very likely to be sending from an IP address (how you connect to the internet) within your office (if that is where your CRM system is set up). The problem with this is that you don't have any whitelisting agreements or similar arrangements. A whitelisting agreement is something that basically says, 'we don't send spam and we follow best practice, so please don't block our emails'. These agreements are put in place with internet service providers and other organizations that are on the lookout for spam, and the advantage of using a good ESP is that they will have these in place. The risk is that when you start sending emails, someone thinks you are sending spam so blocks your IP address. Suddenly, no one in your office can send emails at all because they are all getting blocked, and you are not very popular!

> **IP BLACKLISTING**
>
> If you are sending emails from your office IP address, and if this address is seen as suspicious by those organizations looking out for spam, you could get blacklisted. If you are seeing some of your emails not being delivered for some reason and are concerned about the fact that you may have been blacklisted, you can use a free service to check your IP address. If you are blacklisted, you can then contact the organization blocking you and they will have a process that you will need to go through to get unblocked. Visit: http://www.mxtoolbox.com.

The other reason to use an ESP is because of the generally superior functionality they have in regard to email. They will be automatically set up to deal with things such as unsubscribe requests and bounced emails, whereas this may be something you need to set up when sending email via your CRM if it sits on a computer in your office. ESPs also update their functionality on an ongoing basis and offer more reporting than you can get from a CRM system generally.

Data sync

If we have both a CRM and an ESP, the reason they need to be integrated quickly becomes clear when we look at the workflow (see Figure 10.2). We will take some email data from our CRM, build a list in our ESP and send out an email campaign. We will then have some reporting and details of who has unsubscribed in our ESP. Unless we then get this information back into our CRM, we are storing information in two places and there are risks and limitations associated with this. First, there is a risk that we email someone directly from our CRM who has unsubscribed via our ESP – and this is a breach of spam rules in most countries. The other problem is that we then don't have complete data in either system, so our future targeting will be limited.

The solution is to sync back the data we collect in our ESP to our CRM and, as we collect more email data in our CRM, we are able to import into our ESP without duplication. Most ESPs will offer a CRM integration service or provide an API (application programming interface), which means that a third-party developer should be able to do the necessary work.

Figure 10.2 The challenges and reasons for CRM and ESP integration

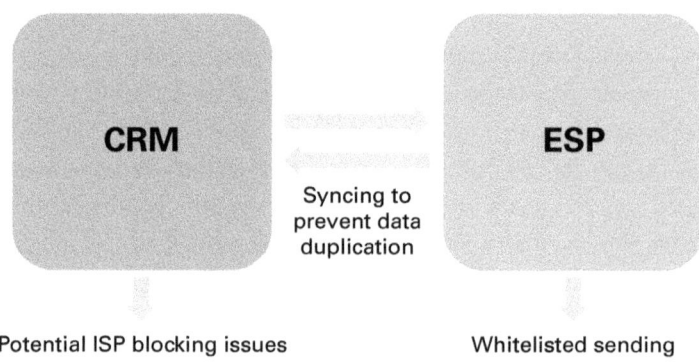

If your CRM and ESP are in the cloud (that is, they are online services rather than something that is installed on a machine in your office), it is generally easier for the systems to speak to each other in real time. Otherwise you may need to do some form of hourly or daily sync. For this reason, if you use something like Salesforce for a CRM and MailChimp for an ESP, both of which are online services and designed to work together, life will be a lot easier.

The alternative and far less ideal solution used by many organizations (because their systems are not integrated) involves importing data from a CRM system and using the ESP to de-duplicate these data. The ESP then works out which email addresses being imported are new, which are duplicates and which have already unsubscribed. However, in this scenario data are not copied back to the CRM, so it is essential that no emails are sent from the CRM directly in case some users have unsubscribed.

If our systems are integrated we can then collect information via our ESP in the form of questionnaires and surveys and use this elsewhere in our marketing efforts via our CRM and in our future email campaigns.

CRM and AI chatbots

For many years we have been able to build automated chatbots into our websites, and for years they have not quite been as useful as we would have liked. Many aspects of 'conversational design', the process of trying to make chatbots more useful, were simply setting up a series of rules. If someone mentions phrase A, then give response B, and so on. And even with the greatest planning in the world, we would never be able to plan for every potential question or situation.

With the huge growth in generative artificial intelligence (AI) and the large language models these are based on, we can now create chatbots that are not only far more adept at having more human conversations but can also be trained in our tone of voice and even give repositories of information such as our product catalogues, frequently asked questions and technical support libraries. This combination of AI-driven chat, combined with our own data, is a powerful combination that can make chatbots hugely more intuitive and effective to interact with.

Free tools like https://chatspot.ai/ from Hubspot show what is already easily possible, and as these tools evolve, we will see an increasing focus on replacing current aspects of our brand experience with more intuitive chat and voice interfaces.

Advanced personalization and triggering

Many ESPs actually offer services similar to that provided by a CRM, allowing you to add many fields of data against a particular email address for segmenting and personalizing your emails (this can mean there is sometimes a bit of blurring between functionality offered by either system). The more advanced ESPs will allow you to integrate your email system with your website so that you can look at visitor behaviour. They can trigger emails based on all this different information and dynamically generate emails according to rules that you set.

Marketing automation

Marketing automation takes this idea of automatically triggering certain emails (or other forms of outbound communications) a stage further by trying to align it more closely with the sales process and adding the idea of lead nurturing and qualification. Once again, this kind of directly sales-related marketing would not generally be associated with branding but, as we have said, digital branding is created by the sum of every touchpoint someone has with your organization or product, and automation allows us to shape those touchpoints into a cohesive and personalized process. Some of the more advanced CRM systems are actually fully fledged automation platforms as well.

Figure 10.3 Marketing automation is used in the nurturing and qualification stage of the sales and marketing process

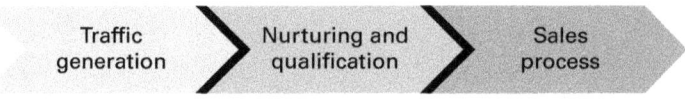

The lead nurturing process

So, let's clarify exactly where marketing automation can fit and where it is and isn't useful. It is generally used when the buying cycle of a product is long or complex. The idea is that we are able to understand where someone is in the buying process, what their current motivation is, and therefore understand what the next steps should be. The next steps may be triggering some form of outbound communications such as an email, or we may decide that this person is now a qualified sales lead, and we hand over to the sales team.

Marketing automation is all about nurturing and then qualifying sales leads via a marketing program in order to increase the quantity and quality of leads we generate and, in turn, sales (see Figure 10.3).

Automation scoring

At the heart of most automation systems is the concept of scoring. This scoring is used to qualify potential sales leads and decide when to trigger particular pieces of content. The scoring can be made up of a number of different factors, as highlighted below, and each system approaches things slightly differently. However, the core idea is that when a particular scoring threshold is reached an action is triggered.

MARKETING AUTOMATION SYSTEMS AND RESOURCES

There are a lot of marketing automation providers out there and the market can be complicated and confusing on first inspection. The three companies below all offer excellent marketing automation systems, and they also provide huge amounts of educational resources on the topic on their websites:

- Marketo: **http://www.marketo.com**
- Eloqua: **https://www.oracle.com/cx/marketing/automation/**
- Hubspot: **http://www.hubspot.com**

Implicit scores

Implicit scores are based on behaviour. We have highlighted a few of the potential behaviours that can be used to help with marketing automation, but remember that in order to use all these different measures, the systems that collect this information will need to be integrated with your automation system:

- Website behaviour:
  - pages looked at;
  - duration of visit;
  - downloads;
  - registration;
  - tools used.
- Events:
  - registration;
  - attendance;
  - sessions attended;
  - stands visited.
- Webinar:
  - registration;
  - attendance;
  - voting;
  - questions asked.
- Email:
  - opens;
  - clicks;
  - content clicked on.

- Social media:
  - likes/follows/+1s;
  - comments;
  - shares.

Explicit scores

Explicit scores are based on the information we hold about an individual or organization:

- Individual:
  - job role;
  - experience;
  - buying power;
  - location;
  - social influence;
  - demographics.
- Organization:
  - size;
  - revenue;
  - industry;
  - location;
  - relationship (customer, lead, partner).

Weighting

Each of these scores can then be weighted to decide how important they are to you or not. For example, the size of your company may matter to me very little, but your job title may be very important. The weighting will have an impact on when an action is triggered, so getting weighting right is essential to an effective automation campaign; we discuss below how your scoring and weighting will be adjusted and improved on an ongoing basis.

Negative scores

There may also be factors that we use to reduce scores. This can include implicit activities such as unsubscribing from an email list or leaving a negative review or comment in social media.

At this stage, we also need to factor in time. For example, say you had visited my website, looked at some content, downloaded some things and that this had been sufficient to trigger a sales email, but you then don't follow up or visit my website again in the next month. Once that month has passed, should you then get another sales email? The answer is probably no, and we can protect ourselves from these kinds of situations by adding in automatic time-based score degradation. What we are doing is basically saying that you score points for certain things, but those things only indicate your interest or intent for a limited period of time, and we therefore lower the scores gradually over time.

More advanced automation options

So far we have looked at scoring an individual based on their behaviour, or information we know about them. However, in certain circumstances we may want to consider more advanced ways of analysing behaviour. For example, say I have a high-cost product that is complicated to buy. If I see an individual visit my web page for this product once or twice that may not be enough to trigger a follow-up. However, if 10 people at the same organization have each been looking at this product I would almost certainly want to follow up. So, by setting rules at an individual level and an organizational level I can spot this happening.

Different automation systems will offer different functionalities to achieve things such as the example just outlined. It is therefore always good to try to map out what kind of behaviours you are trying to identify before choosing a provider, so that you can make sure they offer the functionality you need.

Testing, learning and adjusting

A key element of any successful marketing automation project will be in getting your rules, scoring and weighting right so that you are nurturing leads and passing high-quality leads to sales. To do this, there are a few factors we need to consider.

One of the keys to a successful marketing automation project is to make sure both marketing and sales people are involved throughout the process of defining, scoring and weighting thresholds. You can generate all the leads you want, but if the quality is not high enough, none will convert and the process will have been a waste of time.

In order to build effective rules in the first place, a good starting point is to take a sale that you have already won and work backwards with the data you have. Would they have met your scoring criteria? If not, you clearly need to adjust things. This is known as a pre-deployment test. Once your rules are in place and the system is up and running, you can take a sample of the leads that you have qualified and passed to sales and see how many converted into actual sales. If they didn't, you need to examine your rules and see if they need adjusting to improve the quality of the leads. This is a post-deployment test.

A warning on marketing automation

On paper, marketing automation sounds like a great idea and the key principles are straightforward. However, achieving this in reality is not always easy. First, most of the systems involved are quite costly and the set-up process is something you will most likely need help with. This means there will be an initial set-up cost and project in most cases. If the systems that you use for email, website content management and CRM are not directly compatible with your automation system, you are likely to have some initial integration challenges. Once these are overcome – and you shouldn't underestimate how difficult this can be to achieve – you need to define your rules. This can be time-consuming and complicated, may involve lots of people and will need ongoing refinement. Also, this is something that should be considered a long-term plan. I say that from the experience of never having seen an automation project take less than 18 months from beginning to satisfactory outcome, as a lot of issues and challenges tend to be highlighted when you try to implement it.

CRM and automation conclusions

Integrating CRM and marketing systems to achieve a single customer view should be considered essential. It will give you the flexibility and ability to do smart marketing, which is essential to achieve great digital branding. Integration allows you to personalize the experience that your audience will receive and gives you much easier insights into that audience.

Marketing automation, on the other hand, is fantastic when implemented but is only suited to particular scenarios involving complicated products and services. It is a complicated process that needs the proper planning and resourcing to make it work effectively.

It is unusual to explore things like systems, data and infrastructure when discussing branding, but when we define digital branding as the sum of the touchpoints that someone experiences, it soon becomes clear why it has an integral part to play. We only need to take an everyday example to see how integral systems are to the user experience, what we think of a brand and how it can impact our likelihood to purchase. If I browse your website and look at certain products but don't buy them, and you then send me an email listing similar products to those that I have been browsing, this can be an effective form of behavioural targeting. However, if I then buy a product but you continue to market that product to me, it will potentially have a negative impact. Both the positive and negative sides of this are possible because of the systems we use and the way in which we implement them.

From integration to transmedia campaigns 11

Before we move on to Part Three (Digital brand strategy and measurement), this chapter looks at how to bring together the tactical channels and technologies we've discussed to deliver cohesive digital branding.

Integration

It all starts with the idea of integration. We have identified our value proposition, aligned it with the target audience's needs and focused on value throughout. Each of our channels has been carefully selected, and we understand the potential journeys between each of these channels and how this may be a complex and non-linear process. We have identified our content requirements to deliver the optimal journey and delivered this in a frictionless way, regardless of what device or platform our audience is using. So we have integrated digital branding, right? Very nearly.

What is missing is the glue that makes it stick together, which in this case is data. We need to test, learn to refine things and to adjust. The environment we operate in is fast moving and fluid. Therefore our digital branding needs to be fluid and fast to adjust as well. That is why Part Three will be essential in order to create successful digital branding that will adapt and stand the test of time.

Multichannel marketing is dead

Multichannel marketing is the idea of delivering your marketing via multiple channels, which traditionally meant print, TV, catalogues and a website that said the same thing (or some other online/offline mix). It meant, for example, that a special offer on one channel was offered in the same way on another channel.

The reality is that if you are still trying to achieve this you've got it all wrong. Different channels are used differently and we don't want exactly the same from each. Digital means that we have dozens of different channels and we certainly don't want them all to communicate the same things. Yet that is not to say we don't want consistency.

> **CONSISTENCY OF BRAND**
>
> The traditional idea of brand recognition is still essential. You need to be able to recognize my brand easily, so that the efforts I have made via my digital branding to make you understand my value proposition are remembered easily. Without that clear understanding of what the brand represents, the brand recognition is fairly pointless. Consistency in visual identity and tone only serves a purpose if the value you provide is clear.

Omni-channel marketing

Omni-channel marketing recognizes the fact that my target audience will want to engage and communicate with me across multiple channels in a way that suits them. It recognizes that each channel plays a different role in the user journey, and this role may change and adapt according to what the person engaging with it wants.

Bear in mind, though, that each user may start the user journey at a different point and jump many of the steps you expected. They may also revisit certain steps multiple times and leave long durations of time between each step. For example, I know that on average a lead generated on my website is done so by a visitor who has visited around five times. This means they have visited my site again and again, obviously finding something useful each time, before they finally decide to enquire about the service we offer. Without knowing this, I may have dismissed the traffic being sent to my site by various channels, as it never seemed to be converting into business. In reality, I just didn't understand the number of steps and complexity involved. Understanding this omni-channel approach is at the heart of truly understanding how different elements of your marketing efforts are contributing to your digital branding.

The approach to digital branding outlined in this section embraces omni-channel marketing with its focus on user journey and final outcomes.

Transmedia storytelling

I love saying the phrase 'transmedia storytelling' to people. They generally give me a bit of a smirk and then give me an 'I'm not buying any of this nonsense' kind of look, as if I've just expressed the silliest marketing jargon ever invented. However, it is real and is a fantastic opportunity to achieve incredibly powerful digital branding.

In reality, transmedia storytelling goes back to the very beginning of marketing. In fact, it goes back to the very beginning of language and communication. If I tell you a fact, you will probably forget it fairly quickly. However, if I tell you a story that communicates a fact, you'll most likely remember it. It brings it to life, gives it context and makes it engaging. It's human nature, and it's how we've communicated since before we could speak. It's all about narrative.

Transmedia storytelling aims to tie together each of the channels and platforms we use – using narrative. This can lead to extremely memorable and engaging experiences. It also relies on great creative concepts and absolute attention to detail when exploring how the user journey can be understood and managed. Below is an example of one of my favourite transmedia campaigns – gamification.

GAMIFICATION

Gamification is the principle of encouraging behaviours by rewarding a user in some way. This may be as simple as posting a high score to a public leader board (and remember, this doesn't need to be limited to games, it could be for the most technical questions answered, etc). It can also take more complex forms, such as being the first user to discover a piece of hidden content or unlocking hidden features when certain activities are carried out.

The key thing that makes gamification work is that the reward should be valuable to the user. This may be in the form of content or reward, and very often that reward can just be recognition.

For my favourite example of gamification, take a look at the video for Jay-Z's *Decoded* book launch: **https://www.youtube.com/watch?v=XNic4wf8AYg**.

Self-optimizing campaigns

Due to the development of various artificial intelligence (AI) tools and techniques, the future of truly integrated campaigns gets pretty exciting! If we combine our single customer view with all our data joined up, with machine learning capabilities and generative AI, and allow all of these things to work together (which is increasingly possible due to most systems now having application programming interfaces (APIs) that allow them to interact with other tools) we can imagine some very interesting scenarios. How about a website that automatically adjusts its content based on the behaviour of the website visitor and their activity history? Or what about a website that automatically makes conversion rate optimization changes to itself and tests if they are successful? Or what about fully automated marketing that triggers email, website content, chatbot interactions, online ads and social media content, all based on data, and then uses machine learning to optimize for our desired outcomes? What's interesting is that all of these things are already possible using engagement platforms like those provided by Adobe or Optimizely, but the rapid improvements in AI are making them far more effective and a better user experience.

Integration to transmedia conclusions

The key to delivering great digital branding is to see how all of the different experiences that we are delivering fit together, whether that is via search, social media, mobile or any other digital channel.

In order for these to fit together, though, we need to test our assumptions, to adjust as things change and to have a constant commitment to improvement. To do this, we need feedback. This feedback takes the form of analytics, measurement and surveying our results, and that's what Part Three is all about.

PART THREE
Digital brand strategy and measurement

Introduction

What we have covered so far has suggested a new way to think about branding, plus examples of how you can start to implement your digital branding. What we haven't done yet is walk you through what I really believe differentiates traditional branding from digital branding. And bear in mind, your digital branding is almost certain to interact with offline channels as well, so it is not just about the channels being used – it is actually all about a different approach to measurement.

Effective measurement can help differentiate between branding as an excuse for something that can't really be measured, and exactly what role each piece of marketing activity played in the journey through to the completion of the user journey.

The common challenge for measuring the success of any branding activity, whether online or offline, is that our final conversion – be that a sale or completion of some other task – may happen via a channel that is disconnected from our marketing activities, for example, a sale on someone else's website, an order taken over the telephone or a booking made via a third-party supplier.

What we aim to do in this section is show you an effective technique for bridging these gaps between our end objective and our marketing efforts.

This means that we can calculate the ROI of things such as social media, work out how our print campaigns have contributed, and put a value against all those emails we have been sending out. I'm not saying that it's easy, but it's entirely possible.

Traditional brand metrics

We discussed in Part One that brand is measured by asking questions and trying to judge what someone thinks of a brand – and trying to work out what this means with regard to potential sales.

There are many different ways of looking at this, but generally we would take some sort of sample survey of our audience and see what their attitudes were before and after exposure to some form of marketing. This survey would ask a range of questions, and there are lots of different approaches, but fundamentally we are looking to answer these questions:

- Are you aware of the brand?
- Do you like the brand?
- Do you intend to buy the brand?
- If you have purchased, do you intend to do it again?

Essentially we are assuming that if we can get more people to answer positively to each of these questions, we are likely to get more sales.

What we can now do is take all of the data we have from web analytics and measurement tools, and combine it with traditional surveying techniques to create a feedback process that allows us to continuously improve our marketing activity.

Sum of all experiences

If our digital branding is the sum of all experiences that someone has with our product/service/organization, then we should be able to look at how each experience has impacted the outcome of that overall experience. In this section we look at carrying out the following steps so that we can implement and improve effective digital branding:

- create a digital branding dashboard;
- bring in data from analytics and other sources;
- understand traffic sources and interactions;
- bridge the gap between online activity, offline activity and business outcomes;
- profile and improve.

> **EXAMPLES AND SUPPORTING TEMPLATES**
>
> We have created a number of templates and guidelines to help you implement your digital branding measurement. The most important of these for this section is the digital strategy measurement framework. On our website, we are always adding more case studies and stories of the challenges and successes of implementing the approaches outlined in this section. Most importantly, you'll find an example digital branding dashboard that you can use as a starting point and adjust to your needs. You'll find it all at: **https://www.targetinternet.com/digitalbranding.**

12
Measuring digital branding

The traditional methods for calculating brand value generally make assumptions about the impact that the branding is having on some aspect of your sales. Many of these models are highly complex and not very easy to take action from. What we need to build is a framework that allows us to see the value of each of the pieces of our branding and gain insights that can be actioned to improve things.

Defining brand value and valuation

We need to be very clear what we are talking about if we discuss brand value or valuation. We are not talking about the value of a brand that is put onto the accounts of a business. It is actually about understanding the effectiveness of your marketing and how the different parts contribute, more than it is about valuing a theoretical concept of a brand. We can, however, use this technique in combination with more traditional brand valuation techniques to either come up with more accurate figures or, if nothing else, prove their accuracy in a straightforward way.

Understand the value of every marketing activity

What I am suggesting here is that we should be able to calculate the value of every bit of our marketing activity and look at how it is contributing to the bottom line. This may not be a 100 per cent perfect approach, but it is a lot closer to reality than how we've been doing things up until now (if we've been doing any calculations at all). Those elements we called 'brand building' in the traditional sense basically meant that we didn't really know how much they contributed to the bottom line, but we were pretty sure they did.

Here I suggest a very practical combination of techniques that map out all of the steps of the user journey and see how they contribute to our end objectives. That way, every step is understood and nothing needs to be labelled as brand building. We are simply looking at different stages of our marketing activity and working out what brand impact it has.

For perfection we need a mind-reading device

A perfect approach to marketing is impossible, unless we can mind read. This is because even using surveying techniques, when you ask someone questions about why they did something they often have no idea or recall things incorrectly. For example, if you ask someone why they buy a particular detergent, they probably have no idea. We can put this down to branding, but it still doesn't give us any detailed information. As long as there are humans involved, we try to read minds to some extent.

Digital shot itself in the foot

One of digital's greatest problems has been self-inflicted. In the heady days when digital marketing first started, we happily claimed that everything could be measured and that traditional offline marketing was dead. This was a little arrogant, to say the least. You can measure everything if it ALL happens online. So if you only market online and you make a sale online with a credit card, then you can measure most things. What it doesn't take into account is a scenario such as: the only reason your customer searched and found you on Google in the first place was because their friend told them about you in the pub the night before. Try to measure that. While we still have these kinds of problems with digital, we can nonetheless now measure a lot more than just pure online transactions.

Moving to a cookieless world

Let's start by clarifying something. Cookies, small data files used to track online user behaviours, are not disappearing. It's not going to be a 'cookieless world' but rather a 'third party cookieless world'. But since that doesn't have quite the same ring to it, the marketing world has stuck with 'cookieless'!

For decades, cookies have been key to digital marketing, enabling targeted advertising, personalization and robust analytics. They've been instrumental in mapping user journeys, understanding preferences and delivering tailored experiences. However, this convenience has come at a cost in some cases – diminished user privacy. The 'cookieless' future is not just a challenge but an opportunity for marketers to adopt more transparent, ethical and effective targeting strategies.

Brief history of cookies in digital marketing

Cookies emerged as an internet innovation in the mid-1990s, initially designed to enhance user experience by remembering login information and other preferences. However, they quickly became a powerful tool for digital marketers. Third-party cookies, in particular, allowed for the tracking of users across multiple sites, facilitating a new level of user behaviour analysis and ad targeting. This capability turned cookies into a key aspect of digital advertising, enabling practices like retargeting, where ads follow users across the web, based on their browsing history.

Yet, this power raised concerns. As users became more aware of their digital footprints and the potential misuse of their data, a pushback began. This led to regulatory actions and a growing demand for greater transparency and control over personal data. The response from major tech companies has been significant, with key players like Apple and Google announcing plans to phase out third-party cookies in their browsers. This move marks the beginning of a new, more privacy-focused landscape.

Developing a first-party data strategy

In a 'cookieless' world, first-party data becomes invaluable. This data, collected directly from your audience through interactions with your brand, is both more reliable and more respectful of user privacy. Strategies include encouraging users to log in for a personalized experience, integrating offline and online data, and leveraging email marketing with explicit consent. To do this effectively we need joined up data and systems. This requires our website content management systems, our email service providers and our customer relationship management systems to be fully integrated. This integration has long been a problem in marketing, and for many, the move to first party data has created a burning platform for movement towards joined up systems and data.

Regulations and consumer attitudes

This shift is largely influenced by evolving privacy regulations and changing consumer attitudes towards data privacy. Regulations like GDPR in Europe and CCPA in California have set new standards for data collection and user consent. Consumers are increasingly aware of their digital rights and are demanding more control over their personal data. This changing landscape necessitates a greater focus on transparency and user trust, and for many this will necessitate a major investment in the systems and integration that enable this.

TV has culture, digital doesn't

If you spend a few million pounds on a TV campaign, you're probably quite likely to spend some money on finding out what it did for you. And, in fact, many agencies that work on TV will factor in some calculating of the effectiveness of your campaign into your overall costs. To be fair, if you're spending £2 million on a campaign, £10,000 doesn't seem like much to spend on calculating value. However, if you are spending £500 on a digital campaign, you're not going to spend the same again on finding out if you got return on investment (ROI), because even if you did, you won't have done once you pay to work it out!

So we need to develop a culture of starting out with the concept that all digital activity will be measured – and that we can do this relatively easily and in a cost-effective way.

Filling the gaps

The most important thing we are trying to do in this final part of the book is to fill in some gaps. Does positive engagement actually lead to sales? We assume so but we don't actually know. Does more people being aware of your brand values mean you sell more? We assume so but not necessarily. We will try to fill these gaps by demonstrating how measurement – and asking questions – can provide the answers.

Abandoning volume

One of the key problems with looking at volume-based metrics is that they don't give you an indication of what success actually looks like. You may feel that getting 10,000 followers on your Facebook page is a great success. However, if your nearest competitor has 500,000 followers, it's suddenly a very different story.

Volume is prevalent in social media measurement but also in other digital channels. We look at things such as how many emails we have sent, or the number of page impressions or unique visitors to our websites. These are not so much a measurement of success or failure but rather indicating factors that can lead to our actual desired outcomes.

Benchmarked social measures

To get away from purely focusing on volume-based measurement in social media we can do a number of things, and in the next chapter we look at an approach that ties in web analytics. However, even without getting into analytics we can do some simple things to give us much more practical information. We need to try to benchmark our measurement, and there are a couple of ratio-based social media measures that are easy to use (but fairly rarely used). In order to calculate both of these measures you need two of the social media measurement tools we discussed in Chapter 5: share of voice and audience engagement.

Share of voice is a great ratio for understanding where you sit in relation to your competitors, and for judging the success and reaction to your social media efforts. You will need a social media listening tool to calculate this, and for many channels there are free tools that will do the job.

You start by measuring the total level of conversation around the topic area you are concerned with. For example, a recent client of mine looked at the conversation around skin care. The easiest way to do this is to look at one channel at a time. So, for example, how many tweets there are around the topic of skin care within a particular geographic region (you can do this using the Twitter advanced search).

You achieve this by deciding on a set of keywords and phrases that you want to monitor, and then see the level of conversation on these phrases. You then repeat this process, but just identify the tweets that were specifically about (or mentioning) your product, brand or service. You will then have two numbers: one for total conversations and the other for conversations about your product. Divide the number of conversations about your product by the total number of conversations on the topic, and you have your 'share of voice' percentage. This may be very low, but you can continue your social media efforts and then take the measurement on a regular basis (normally monthly is sufficient). Progress made in increasing this percentage gives you a more useful guide than just looking at the number of tweets or likes. The other great thing about this measure is that you can calculate it for your competitors. You then have a benchmarked measure that can give you an indication of how effective your efforts are, and how that compares to your competitors.

Audience engagement is another percentage that you can easily measure and benchmark against your competitors. I tend to look at it on a platform-by-platform basis so that I know my audience engagement for Twitter, Facebook, Google+, etc and can make efforts to improve this. Again, I normally measure this on a monthly basis.

You start by looking at the size of your overall audience on a particular social platform, such as Facebook or Twitter, and then consider how much of that audience is actually engaging with you. So, for example, if you have 10,000 likes on Facebook, and when you post some content you get 1,000 likes on that piece of content from your likes, then your audience engagement is 10 per cent.

We need to define what we mean by engagement. On a platform like Facebook there are multiple ways to engage as you can like, share and comment on a post. I would count any of these activities as engagement. With Twitter I consider a reply or a re-tweet to be engagement, and so on. Technically speaking, if the same user were to carry out multiple engagement activities on the same platform on the same piece of content, we should probably not count these more than once. In practice, however, it doesn't actually matter as long as you are comparing like for like. As well as taking this measure for your own social platforms, you can very easily analyse your competitors as well.

Benchmarking and business results

Although benchmarked measures don't relate directly to business results, they are far more connected to helping us achieve our objectives than just looking at volume-based metrics alone. Realistically, if you are targeting the right audience your share of voice is growing and your audience engagement is increasing – thus you are in a strong position. There is still a gap between this and actual sales, but we are getting closer.

The next stage is to connect these social media measures to our web analytics and business objectives, which we look at in the next chapters.

Measurement comes in many forms

We need to combine a number of different measurement techniques in order to really understand the impact of each piece of our marketing activity. This includes using basic web analytics, external search volume tools, marketing attribution tools and, finally, chopping up some data in spreadsheets. It is not as painful as it sounds, but the reality is that neither is it easy nor something that most marketers know how to do. This is one of the fundamental issues surrounding calculating ROI that we need to be clear on. It needs to be planned from the outset and is a process we need to repeat and improve.

VIEWPOINTS
Target Internet

Dealing with fake engagement and spam bots

What exactly are social media spam bots, who is behind them, and why are they used to create fake engagements on social content? Let's get to the bottom of this strange online phenomenon.

Figure 12.1 shows a post on Target Internet's Facebook page. Look at all those engagements! What are we getting so spectacularly right?

Well, it's actually very hard for us to tell what we're getting right and what we're getting wrong in our social media strategy because most of the likes and comments on this and many of our other posts can be traced back to social media spam bots. On the surface this might seem like a good thing for us – who could complain about all those easily earned likes and comments?

Digital brand strategy and measurement

Figure 12.1   Fake engagement on a Facebook page

In fact, fake social engagements are a real thorn in our side. For one thing, they clearly are not real comments: 'Anything about this is important' says 'University of Internet Marketing'. Comments like these do nothing in terms of enhancing our representation or stimulating positive dialogue on our channels.

We would much rather have a modest number of great genuine engagements with our content than such a large number of fake ones. Fake engagements skew our social data, which makes it far harder for us to work out which posts are genuinely getting the best reaction from our legitimate followers.

Why is this happening?

Social spam bots exist to earn people followers, sales leads and, ultimately, money. These bots are really just algorithms used in conjunction with social media profiles to create engagements with other people's content. This, in turn, attracts engagement with the profile linked to the algorithm, from both real users and other bots.

Bots will often specifically target content or users with some connection to whatever it is they are ultimately trying to sell. So Target Internet's page is a magnet for B2B digital marketing bots, while singletons might find themselves targeted by bots posing as remarkably amorous social users with supermodel looks.

Why is this happening on social media?

Where other public parts of the web have enjoyed recent wins in their battles with spam content, social media remains a playground for spammers. Think of Google's success in cracking down on spammy links; think of recent improvements to spam comment detection on blogging platforms; and then compare that with the situation on Instagram, where 1 in 10 accounts are thought to be fake! (Kicksta, 2024).

The beauty of X and Instagram is that they give people a platform to say just about whatever they want. Unfortunately, and in spite of legal and practical countermeasures such as spam detection through machine learning, this policy gives spammers a better chance to operate successfully than they might find on more tightly regulated parts of the web.

Primaries and indicators   13

In order to do any effective digital branding we need to understand our potential audience's journey and understand how this can be influenced, improved and essentially lead to our desired outcomes. To do this we need to measure what is important – and learn from this and improve.

Beyond the last click

Analytics (explored in the next chapter) allows us to see activity on our websites and apps, and where that traffic has come from. It also allows us to track our desired outcomes, at least to some extent. What we need to be clear on from the outset, however, are the limitations of analytics and what it can't tell us.

Generally, web analytics takes a 'last click' approach. This means we look at some form of activity, such as a download, and see where the traffic came from that directly preceded the download. What this doesn't tell us are all the steps before that last step. Just because I came to your website from a search engine and then downloaded something doesn't mean the search engine was solely responsible for the download. I may have visited your website 10 times before, from multiple sources over an extended period of time. This is what we really need to understand. Thankfully, by using some relatively new features in tools such as Google Analytics, and in particular its latest version Google Analytics 4 (GA4), this has become a lot easier.

Analytics also can't measure when our outcomes happen offline, such as when our sales come in over the phone or at a showroom. Does this mean that tracking in analytics is a waste of time? Not at all, it just means we need to be clear on what we want to achieve online and that this should be as close as possible to our actual desired outcomes. I define these online goals – that may not be our actual business objective but are as close as we can measure online – as 'primaries'.

As we look at the wide range of measurements we can take from analytics, surveying and other sources that we look at in the rest of Part Three, we need to decide what is important and what is not so important. I like to refer to these different types of online goals and measures as 'primaries' and 'indicators'.

Primaries are the key things that we can monitor online that are as close as possible to our business objectives. If you sell online with a credit card facility, then your 'primary' will be a sale. However, if you are looking for leads it may be forms submitted or calls made to a web-advertised telephone number. It could also be the registration for an event or the download of a very relevant piece of content. These are not our absolute business objectives in many cases but the closest we can come online to achieving these. We will bridge the gap between these activities and our final objectives in Chapters 14 and 15.

Indicators are the things we can measure online that impact how many primaries are completed. In order to get a filled-in lead form, I need website traffic. In order to get that traffic, I need a traffic source (such as a search engine or social media site). For the search traffic, I need to be ranking for certain search terms. For social media I need an engaged audience. Each of these things can be broken down into 'indicators'. For search traffic, my indicators might be as shown in Tables 13.1 and 13.2.

Table 13.1 Indicators and data sources for search traffic

Indicator	Source
Traffic from search engine	Web analytics
Rankings for search terms in search engine	Web ranking tool
Page authority	SEO authority tool
Volume of searches for particular search term	Search engine data

Table 13.2 Indicators and data sources for social traffic

Indicator	Source
Traffic from social platform	Web analytics
Percentage of engaged users	Social platform
Size of audience	Social platform

Figure 13.1 Dashboard showing a 'primary' and 'indicators'

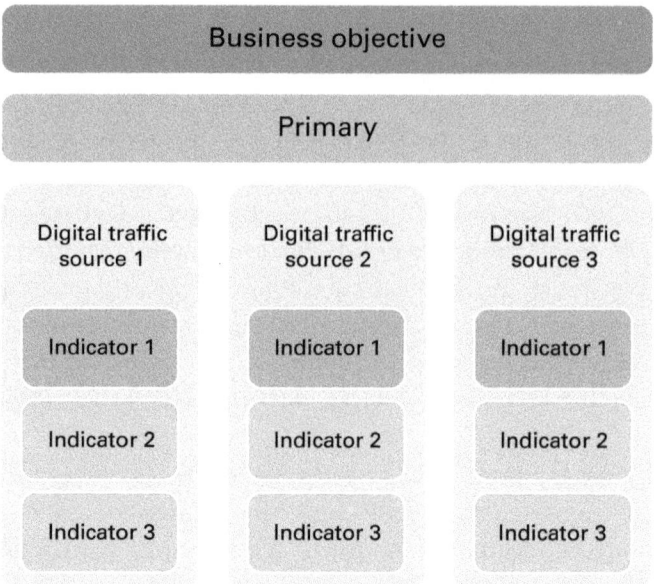

Digital branding dashboards

Each of these indicators takes us further towards our primary, and by bringing them together in a dashboard we can start to see where our challenges may be. Figure 13.1 shows how a single primary can have a number of different indicators and how these can be grouped by traffic source. We will explore where these data come from in the next chapter on analytics and extend this dashboard to include indications of how the channels worked together to achieve our primaries.

> **DASHBOARDS AND MEASUREMENT**
>
> In order to properly measure and improve our digital branding efforts we need to measure the right things. To help with this we have created a digital strategy measurement dashboard that can help you work out what to measure and what is important. It will also help you to work out what is of primary importance and what is just an indicator.
> See **http://www.targetinternet.com/digitalbranding**.

The role of analytics

14

In this chapter we explore the huge opportunity that web analytics gives us and how we use this as part of our digital branding dashboards. Web analytics means you will no longer have the problem of not having enough data with which to assess your campaigns. Your problem now will be having too much data and not knowing what to do with it. In most organizations I look at, they now have web analytics (this is an improvement on a couple of years ago), but the data are not used in an effective way. In fact, the most use that web analytics gets in the majority of organizations is a chart being held up once a month showing web traffic going up. This doesn't say why traffic is going up, how it could be improved further or if, in fact, it is going up more slowly than the competitors. The data are just the starting point. To create effective digital branding we need to be able to analyse those data and use the data to measure and improve our efforts.

Introduction to Google Analytics 4

Google Analytics, a free tool with over 83 per cent global share of the analytics market (W³Techs, 2024), has built-in reports as well as a huge variety of customization options. Its latest incarnation, Google Analytics 4 (GA4), is regularly updated and offers a great deal of what many commercial analytics packages offer (and more in some cases). So one of the most common questions asked is: why is it free?

Google Analytics started out as a commercial tool called Urchin. This was then purchased by Google, repackaged and given away for free to help website owners improve their sites and drive revenue. Why does Google want you to make more money? Because then you are more likely to spend money on their advertising products, which generate more than 80 per cent of their income (Alphabet, 2024).

There is, in fact, a paid version of Google Analytics – Google Analytics 360 – that gives you some of the things absent from the free version, such as an account manager, telephone support and Service Level Agreements. It also gives you even more functionality and extended access to data and customization. However, it costs US $150,000 per year (this may seem like a huge amount but actually represents good value when you consider what you get and the fact it is aimed at enterprise-level organizations).

THE LAUNCH OF GA4

The role of the latest version of Google Analytics seemed to catch marketers off-guard. Even though we were given more than a year's notice of the demise of Universal Analytics (UA), GA4's predecessor, many marketers were caught out and found themselves without year-on-year data, having no effective goals set up (now called key events), and not being entirely sure their accounts were set up properly and whether or not they could therefore trust the new data they had.

To make things worse, GA4 has a small fraction of the reports that UA had, and the interface seems less intuitive. Other features, like the fact the setup wizard didn't automatically tick things off as you completed them, and you had to manually tell GA4 that you had done something in GA4, didn't fill people with confidence. Add the fact that some core settings were hidden away in deeply buried sub-menus, and that some menus have changed place over recent months, has just switched some marketers away from GA4 completely to either seek alternatives or to just bury their heads in the sand and continue with no effective web analytics.

Even with all this in mind, I am going to try and persuade you that, in reality, GA4 is a far superior web analytics solution to UA, and, in fact, it marks a huge leap forward for marketers! So, let's start with the most important points. GA4 is much better equipped for a more privacy-focused world. It doesn't rely on third-party cookies (which are being blocked in more and more places) and has much more granular privacy settings. Beyond this, which is clearly good for our website users, but perhaps doesn't feel of much benefit to marketers, it offers a whole new level of measurement that was previously hard to set up and required the involvement of a developer.

All the activities of our websites or apps are now events, whether that's a page being loaded or a user starting a session (essentially a visit to our website). The great thing is that GA4 goes well beyond pages simply loading and users starting sessions. We now have a huge level of detail on what they are doing within our pages. Whether that is scrolling, starting or completing a form, downloading a PDF or clicking to an external website, all of these things are now tracked as standard (assuming we have Enhanced Measurement switched on). This means we suddenly have a huge amount more potential insight than we ever had in UA out of the box.

The other, and probably most important, aspect of GA4 is that beyond some core reports, it's not really about what is provided as standard. It's all about customizing the standard reports, building completely custom reports and, in fact, changing the menus to our specific requirements. By using the Report Customization, Explore and Library tools we can do all of these things quite easily.

So where should you get started? The most important thing is to make sure that your key events are set up, and this is certainly not as intuitive as it used to be in UA, but once you get your head round it, it will also make many others aspects of GA4 much clearer. We'll explore this more in a moment. To assist with this, we've built a bite-size interactive course on the topic completely free for readers, and you can access it here without an email or any other login details: https://targetinternet.com/freega4.

Throughout this chapter we focus on showing how you can use a tool like Google Analytics to help with every stage of your digital branding. We look at using the tools in practice and understanding how they can be used within our mobile sites and apps.

Setting up analytics

Most analytics packages use a technique called 'page tagging'. When you register for a Google Analytics account, you are given a unique code that needs to be put on every page of your website. This is either done directly using your content management system (CMS), by getting a developer to add the code or by using another tool like Google Tag Manager. This code then sends information back to Google each time someone uses one of your website pages or app screens (see the following box for more on analytics in apps).

> **ANALYTICS DATA**
>
> GA4 is designed to be useful for both websites and apps, much more so than UA ever was. This is because of the automatic tracking of events, that is things that happen within pages, not just the loading of pages themselves. This can include things like scrolling, playing videos and clicking onto PDFs – all things that required extra code in UA.
>
> Another big advantage is the ability to export data from GA4 into BigQuery, where you can do more advanced analysis and even combine with other data.

Core reports

Once you have your analytics code in place, your analytics package will start recording visitors to your website or app. These reports are broken down into a number of different categories, of which some of the core areas are highlighted below.

Reports

The core reports section of GA4 is where you will find the pre-build reports, broken down into four key areas. The big surprise for users of previous versions of Google Analytics, is how few reports there are. The reality is that you can customize any of these reports to show you any data you wanted in pretty much whatever format you want, so the key opportunity here is customization.

The key sections of reports are:

1. Real-time

- Overview: Displays live data about active users on your site/app, including their location, the current pages/screens that they are viewing and events triggered.

2. Life cycle

a. Acquisition

- Overview: Summarizes how users arrive at your site/app, highlighting different channels such as organic search, paid search, social and referrals.

- User acquisition: Focuses on new users, showing metrics like new users, average engagement time and conversions based on their acquisition source.
- Traffic acquisition: Displays data on sessions, showing how users come to your site/app, including metrics like sessions, engaged sessions and bounce rate.

b. Engagement

- Overview: Provides insights into user interactions, including pages/screens viewed, user engagement metrics and event counts.
- Events: Lists all events triggered by users, along with their occurrence frequency and user engagement.
- Conversions: Highlights important actions defined as conversions, showing metrics related to these key events.
- Pages and screens: Shows data on which pages/screens users are viewing most frequently, along with engagement metrics for each.

c. Monetization

- Overview: Offers a summary of revenue data, including total revenue, purchases and ad revenue.
- Ecommerce purchases: Displays detailed information about ecommerce transactions, products sold and revenue generated.
- In-app purchases: For apps, this report provides the data on in-app purchases, including item names, quantities and revenue.
- Publisher ads: Shows revenue from the ads displayed on your site/app, including ad impressions and ad revenue.

d. Retention

- Overview: Tracks user retention over time, showing metrics such as user retention rate, average retention time and returning users compared to new users.

3. User

a. Demographics

- Overview: Provides demographic information about your users, such as age, gender and interests.
- Demographic details: Delves deeper into specific demographic categories, showing how different segments of users engage with your site/app.

b. Tech

- Overview: Summarizes the technology used by your users, including devices, operating systems and browsers.
- Tech details: Provides detailed information about the technology profiles of your users, such as device model, screen resolution and app version.

As well as these reports you can also connect GA4 to other Google services like Search Console and Google Ads, and bring in some limited data from these platforms to see reporting in one place.

Explore

The Explore section is essentially a custom report building tool. It allows you to bring in all of the data that matter to you and display in a meaningful way. Dimensions, metrics and segments are fundamental concepts that help you analyse and interpret data about your website or app performance. Let's explore each in turn:

Dimensions

Dimensions are descriptive attributes or characteristics of your data. They provide the context for your metrics.
   Examples:

Page title: The title of a webpage.

Device category: The type of device used (eg desktop, tablet, mobile).

Country: The geographic location of the user.

Event name: The name of the event that was triggered.

Dimensions are used to categorize and break down your data. For instance, if you want to know which pages are most popular, you would use the 'Page Title' dimension.

Metrics

Metrics are quantitative measurements. They provide the numbers that you analyse.
   Examples:

Users: The number of unique users who visited your site or app.

Sessions: The total number of sessions (a session is a group of user interactions within a given time frame).

Pageviews: The number of times a page was viewed.

Event count: The number of times an event occurred.

Metrics are used to measure performance. For example, you might look at the 'Users' metric to see how many people visited your site over a specific period.

Segments

Segments are subsets of your data. They allow you to isolate and analyse specific parts of your data.
   Examples:

New users segment: Users who are visiting your site for the first time.

Returning users segment: Users who have visited your site before.

Geographic segment: Users from a specific country or region.

Behaviour segment: Users who completed a specific action, like making a purchase or signing up for a newsletter.

Segments help you focus on specific user groups to understand their behaviour better. For example, you might create a segment for users who made a purchase to analyse their journey through your site and optimize the conversion path.

How they work together

You can combine dimensions and metrics to create a detailed analysis. For instance, you might want to see the number of pageviews (metric) for each page title (dimension). By applying segments, you can focus on specific groups within your dimensions and metrics. For example, you might apply a segment for mobile users to see how many sessions (metric) originated from mobile devices (dimension) (Figure 14.1).

Advertising

The Advertising reports in GA4 are very badly named. They are, in fact, the attribution modelling reports and are really important for measuring our branding efforts. They are called Advertising here, as Google would like you to use them to attribute value to the advertising that you carry out, particularly the advertising you do with them! However, they are a brilliant set of reports for understanding how each visit to our website contributed toward our desired outcomes. We'll look at attribution modelling reports more in a moment.

Figure 14.1 The custom report builder in GA4

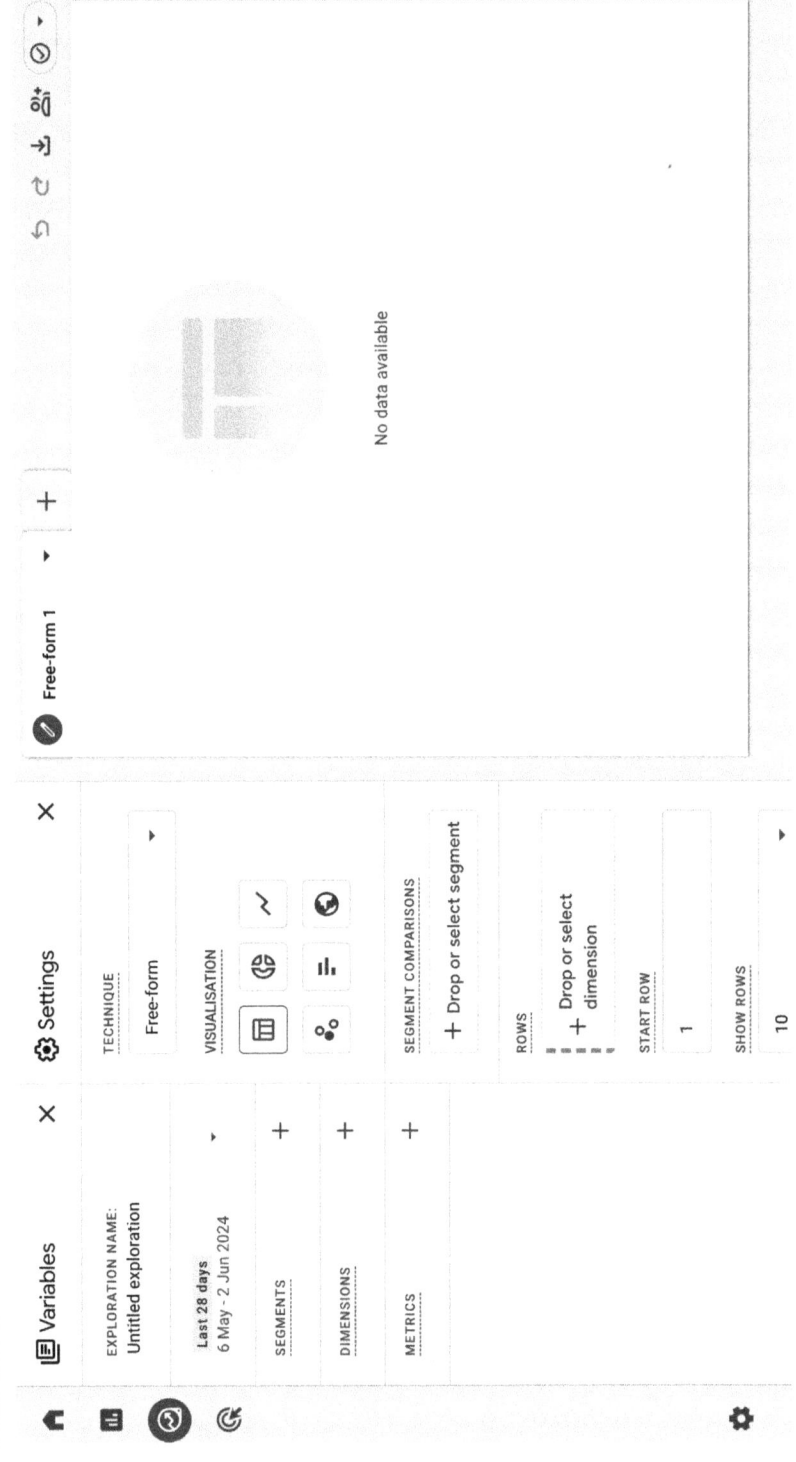

(Google and the Google logo are registered trademarks of Google Inc, used with permission)

COMPARISONS AND UNDERSTANDING THE USER JOURNEY

Comparison is an often missed but hugely powerful feature of Google Analytics that is incredibly useful when trying to understand the user journey and each touchpoint of your digital branding. It allows you to select a particular segment of your audience and then see all of the normal reports for that particular segment. You can also select multiple segments and compare these on the same report. There are predefined segments that you can easily select, or with a little knowledge you can build your own custom comparisons.

NOT ALL BOUNCES ARE EQUAL

We generally assume a bounce is a bad thing. For example, someone arriving at your website from a search engine, landing on your home page, not liking the look of it and then leaving, is a bounce. However, someone bookmarking your blog because they read it every week, landing on your blog page, reading it for 25 minutes and then leaving, is also a bounce. The visitor still entered and exited your website on the same page. Therefore, a bounce isn't always a bad thing if the user has got what they wanted. For this reason you will see fewer bounce rates and more 'engagement' metrics in GA4, meaning that someone has engaged with your page for more than a defined period of time (which as standard in GA4 is 10 seconds).

Key events

By understanding what our primary objective is we can then set this up as a goal in our web analytics. In GA4 our goals are known as key events. This means we have a direct measure of the success of any digital activity we are carrying out. It's fundamental at this stage to understand the different type of analytics key events and work out how to set these up properly.

A key event can be anything from somebody submitting a form, scrolling to the bottom of a particular page, downloading a PDF or watching a particular video to the end. It is essential we set up our desired primary objective as an analytics key event so that we can access reports that let us see the user journey that lead to that conversion, and which of our digital channels and campaigns contributed. Below you will find a complete interactive guide to setting up GA4 key events:

https://targetinternet.com/resources/free-ga4-course-key-events/

Attribution modelling

One of the limitations of goal reports is that they take a 'last click' approach. This means that if you look at the source of a report it will tell you what traffic source delivered the visitor to your site. For example, if you did a search in Google, came to my site and then filled in a form, the source of the goal would be a search. There is a problem with this, however: for example, if you receive an email, visit my website, then a week later you do a search and then you fill in a form on my website – again the source of the conversion would be given as the search, but clearly the email has also contributed in this instance.

Thankfully, because we have set up our primary objectives as key events, there is a set of reports that does this for us very easily. These are the attribution modelling reports found under the 'Advertising' menu option in GA4.

These attribution modelling reports show us, of all the people that completed our analytics goals, which channels did they use on the way there (and it can look at this over a period of time, up to 90 days currently). Understanding what this is telling us is really important, and the key point is that the channels it shows are not the last thing somebody did before completing our goal but one of the things they did. This is important because a journey through to completing a primary goal may include visiting the website many times and coming in from lots of different places. The report looks at each step in the journey and uses something called a data-driven attribution model that utilizes machine learning (an application of artificial intelligence) to give each step in the journey a weighting score.

> **Hands-on learning resources for analytics**
>
> Reading about analytics is one thing, but when you come to try out each of these reports you may need a little more help. I have listed here my

favourite two analytics learning resources. Both are from Google and both are free:

Analytics Academy: these interactive online tutorials walk you through the core reports of analytics in a very clear way: **https://analytics.google.com/analytics/academy/**.

Analytics Mania YouTube channel: this is an absolute goldmine of analytics tutorials and explanations.: https://www.youtube.com/@AnalyticsMania.

Tracking code

In order to track some sources of traffic through to your site you may need to use analytics tracking code. This can be particularly useful if, for example, you are placing different versions of an ad on different devices. Tracking code is added to a web link and then, when the traffic source is shown, the details you have entered will be given. Let's walk through an example in order to make sense of this.

If I place a link in my email that drives traffic to my website without adding tracking code, the traffic from the email will show up as direct traffic. The reason for this is that when a user clicks on a link in an email, Google doesn't generally know where that click has come from (unless we are talking about webmail). Therefore, to really understand our email visitors we need to add tracking code to all of our links so that we can separate where the traffic has come from and analyse it properly.

Generating traffic code is very straightforward and, thankfully, Google gives us a tool to simplify things. First, search 'Google URL builder'. You will then find the Google URL builder (which is just an online form for generating tracking code). Enter the page you want to link to, fill in a couple of fields and it will generate a new link that includes your original link and appends the tracking code. Now if you add this to your email, when someone clicks on the link it will be reported in Google Analytics as 'campaign traffic' along with the name you gave it and any other details entered into the URL builder.

This can be used to generate tracking code for emails, online ads, links in social media sites and so on, and can help you track a particular link and the traffic it is driving to your site. This is essential when trying to implement digital marketing dashboards, so that we can break down between different social media sites, etc.

Dashboards and analytics

In the previous chapters we explored the idea of using dashboards to better understand our overall digital branding. Much of the data for these dashboards will be found within our analytics, particularly for our primaries (normally set up as key events) and some of our indicators (such as volumes of traffic from a particular source).

We also need to see how these channels have worked together to achieve our primaries, and Figure 14.2 shows how primaries, indicators and data from attribution reports can be combined to visually give us an indication of what is and isn't working. The 'percentage contribution' is taken from our attribution reports to show how each traffic source has contributed to the particular primary we are looking at.

Figure 14.2 This dashboard shows a 'primary' along with a number of 'indicators' as well as showing how the traffic sources have worked together (by using information from attribution modelling reports)

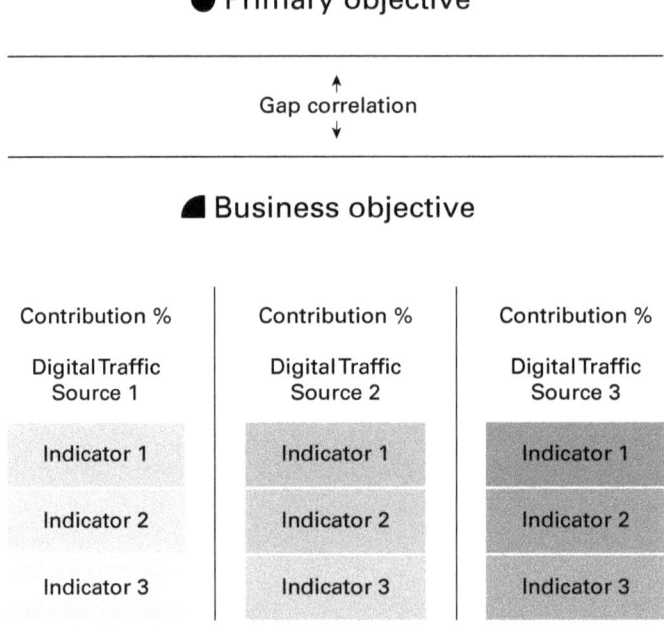

Analytics conclusions

Web analytics gives us a huge array of tools and information with which to better understand our audience and how they are moving towards completing our online objectives. However, unless all of our business is done online, we still need to bridge the gap between online and offline, and understand how our online activities are contributing to our overall business objectives. This is what we will look at in the next chapter.

> **DASHBOARDS AND ANALYTICS TEMPLATE**
>
> Don't forget, we have produced a dashboard framework that you can download in full and adjust to your own requirements to help track and improve your digital branding efforts: **http://www.targetinternet.com/digitalbranding**.

Bridging the gaps

15

The dashboard we built in previous chapters that shows us how each online channel has contributed towards achieving our primaries has some limitations. It doesn't actually tell us how many people who complete our primary actually go on to complete by business objective. Although a primary shows an action that is as close as possible to our final business objective, it doesn't mean this has actually happened. Also, the dashboard so far only factors in online but not any offline experiences.

Gap correlation

Gap correlation is a simple process of asking questions that show us the connection between our primaries and our final business objectives. We ask each of those customers who complete our final business objective if they completed any of our primaries. We then build a percentage, on average, of those who do. We can approach understanding this percentage in two ways: sample data and continuous sampling.

Sample data

We can take a percentage of those customers who complete our final objective and ask them about their primary completion. Once we believe we have taken a large enough sample (take a look at 'Sample size and confidence levels' in the box below for more detail on this) we can then use this percentage going forward to estimate how many people who complete each of our primaries will go on to complete our business objectives.

Continuous sampling

In this scenario, we continuously ask those customers who complete our objectives about their primary completions and feed this into our dashboard.

This is obviously less prone than 'sample data' to giving us misguiding information that has occurred due to a change over time in the relationship between primaries and business objectives.

> **SAMPLE SIZES AND CONFIDENCE LEVELS**
>
> We need to know how many customers we have to ask questions in order to get an accurate estimate of the relationship between primaries and business objectives. The number of customers we ask is our sample size. The larger the percentage of our customers we ask, the more confident we can be of our results. To do this effectively we need to work out what percentage of our overall customers we need to sample. A sample size calculator can help you work out your level of confidence in the data you collect: https://www.calculator.net/sample-size-calculator.html.

Keeping it simple – and the danger of selecting the wrong primaries

This approach to understanding how each of the different elements of our marketing are contributing towards our end objective is supposed to generate an easy-to-use dashboard that can show you what is working and what isn't. It is purposefully simple, but as set out below does not take into account a few factors.

Attribution modelling systems, such as that built into Google Analytics, try to look at the order in which different channels are used in order to work out their contribution. This model bundles together all the different possibilities of sequences of actions in order to try to create an actionable dashboard. Where this can go wrong, however, is when we select the wrong primaries. The risk is that no one is completing these, but they then go on to complete our business objectives. This would leave the dashboard fairly useless. For this reason I suggest focusing on a range of primaries initially so you can see which ones are the most important. You can then filter this down to those that are most suited to a simple dashboard. Remember, the aim of a dashboard when we are looking at digital branding is to understand at a high level how the sum of experiences we are providing is having an impact, rather than getting drowned in the detail.

Bring in offline channels and experiences

An offline experience includes such things as seeing a print ad, watching a TV ad, calling customer support or attending an event. What we need to do is understand how each of these offline experiences impacted the potential customers' 'objective intent'. What this means in practice is that when asked after this offline experience, did they state they were more likely to carry out the action that is our business objective (this is normally a sale but doesn't have to be) or not? The challenging thing here is to work out how to ask the question, and it will depend on what type of offline experience we are talking about. For a call to customer support, this can normally be achieved fairly easily. However, for a TV ad or print ad we need to get more creative, and normally this involves using the ads on a test audience. This test audience should be as close to our target audience as possible, but

Figure 15.1 Extending the dashboard to include the contribution of offline experiences

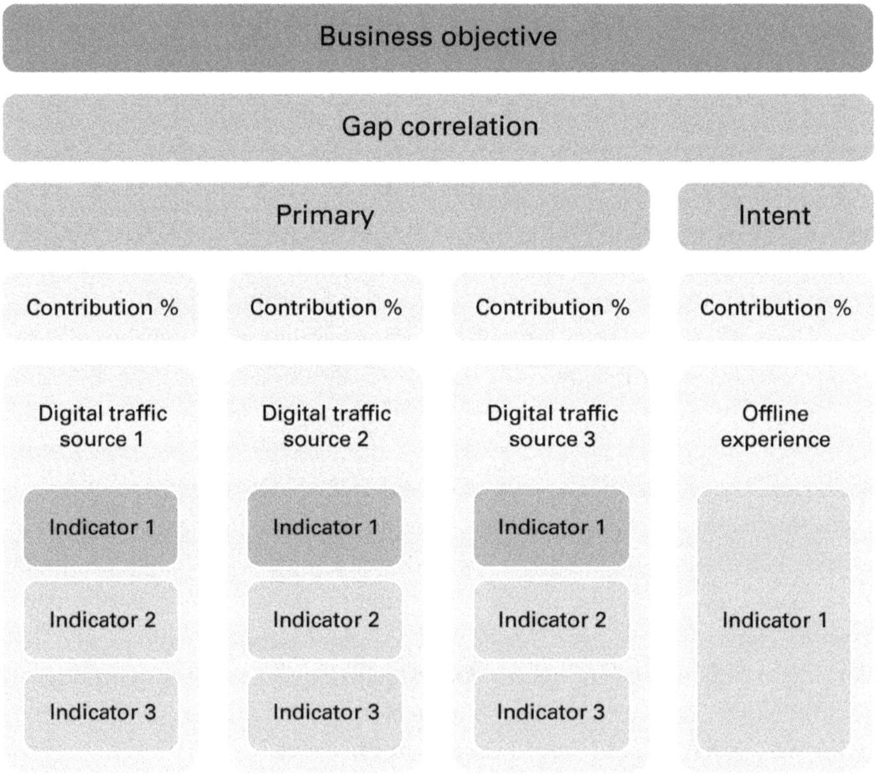

Business objective

Gap correlation

Primary	Intent

Contribution %	Contribution %	Contribution %	Contribution %
Digital traffic source 1	Digital traffic source 2	Digital traffic source 3	Offline experience
Indicator 1	Indicator 1	Indicator 1	
Indicator 2	Indicator 2	Indicator 2	Indicator 1
Indicator 3	Indicator 3	Indicator 3	

the question about buying intent may need to be a hypothetical one: do you think this would increase your likelihood to carry out our objective? For this reason, sampling offline experiences is generally far less accurate than for online ones.

This sampling gives us the 'intent percentage' and, for the sake of simplicity, we are seeing this as equivalent to completing a primary for our online experiences, as shown in Figure 15.1. These two are, again, not a like-for-like example but nevertheless provide a good actionable dashboard.

> **AVOIDING THE NEED FOR OFFLINE SAMPLING**
>
> If the idea of getting together a test audience and asking them questions seems difficult and inaccurate, there is an alternative solution: simply try to drive people from the offline experiences to your website and then get them to complete an online primary.
>
> We can see the flaw in this approach through an example, however. If I see a print ad that encourages me to go online, I then do a search in Google and arrive at your site. We will see this visit as being from Google rather than the print ad. The solution is to get your audience to use a URL specific to the ad (which many just won't do) or when they are completing the primary get them to indicate that they came from the ad – and then track this as a different online goal and therefore a different primary. It is not as simple to set up and you may need to get a developer involved in building custom forms, but it can add more accuracy to your data.

The next thing we need to understand is that of all the people who, after an offline experience, responded that they then had 'objective intent', how many actually went on to carry out this objective. This question can be asked at the same time as we ask about the completion of our online primary. Again, we need a suitable sample size in order to be confident of our results (see the 'Sample sizes and confidence levels' box for more details).

Offline indicators

For online experiences we have a number of indicators and these are normally layered in terms of how they influence each other. For example, we

Figure 15.2 Spreadsheet version of the digital branding dashboard

Objective				Sell service			
Gap correlation							
Primary/Intent		Lead generation form 38%			Intent 22%	Intent 38%	Intent 9% 11%
Contribution %	58%	30%	25%	19%			
Source	Organic search	Paid search	Facebook	Twitter	Event		Print Ad
Measure 1	Search traffic	PPC traffic	Facebook traffic	Twitter traffic	Attendees		Predicted audience
Value 1	8000	652	560	260	197		2500
Measure 2	Top 50 rankings	CTR	Engaged likes	Engaged followers	Registrations		
Value 2	122	3.20%	1,040	768	280		
Measure 3	Site authority	Impressions	Likes	Followers	Enquiries		
Value 3	65%	20,375	13,927	7,940	340		

might have Facebook likes as one indicator, then engaged likes and then, finally, traffic from Facebook. However, with offline experiences we may just have one indicator and generally this will be volume-based. For example, with a print ad we may just use the number of people we expect to see the ad, based on the figure given to us by the publication (or similar for a TV ad). With events and things such as customer service calls we may be able to add more levels of indicators, for example, an event registration followed by event attendance. Again, examples of this can be found in the spreadsheet version of the digital branding dashboard that you can download from our website.

A word on contribution

The contribution percentage shown in Figure 15.1 and in the downloadable spreadsheet needs to be clearly understood. For online it is showing the contribution of each traffic source towards the particular primary. For offline it is showing the contribution percentage towards buying intent. This is not a like-for-like comparison and the percentages of offline/online should not be compared. The aim of the dashboard is to allow us to adjust different elements of our marketing in order to try to improve the results.

If we want to understand the overall contribution of both online and offline together, and do a like-for-like comparison, we need to ask some different questions, as outlined in the next chapter.

Seeing it in action

Figure 15.2 shows the spreadsheet version of the dashboard in action, with a number of online and offline experiences. The spreadsheet includes tips for each sell, explaining what it is indicating and where the opportunities for improvement are.

DASHBOARDS AND MEASUREMENT TEMPLATES

Don't forget, we have produced a dashboard framework that you can download in full and adjust to your own requirements to help track and improve your digital branding efforts. This includes help with tracking the gaps in your measurement framework and calculating the appropriate sample size needed in order to be confident of your gap correlation: **http://www.targetinternet.com/digitalbranding**.

VIEWPOINTS

Rachel Exton, Vice President Marketing, Pearson

Do less, do bigger, do better

One of the many things I threaten to have tattooed on my forehead on a regular basis is 'do less, do bigger, do better'.

Ronseal-esque in its simplicity, most people agree with the approach in principle but many businesses struggle to put it into practice. (Ronseal, a wood stain brand, coined the phrase 'it does what it says on the tin' as a purposeful way of doing no-nonsense marketing. The term grew to be used in many other contexts.)

Overwhelmed by opportunity

Companies, particularly new or growing businesses, tend to take on too many things.

They want to make sure they're grabbing every opportunity, leaving no money on the table.

It's not just campaign-loving marketing departments that are guilty of taking on too much. At an organizational level, businesses tend to have more strategic priorities than their stretched employees can remember.

It's hard to say no to opportunities, but no company – no matter how big they are, no matter their budget or team size – can do it all.

Set up to fail

In the 'grab every opportunity' camp, there's a sense that it's better to try lots of things, that way, you'll know what works.

But juggling too much sets teams and initiatives up to fail. It's skewing the test.

Overly busy teams miss opportunities for collaboration and are stretched too thin to execute brilliantly. Even the best idea in the world can fail if badly executed.

Working really hard yet only being able to deliver mediocre stuff is a recipe for a disengaged team. Engagement dips, performance dips, and it becomes a vicious cycle.

Five is the magic number

That's where my lovely forehead tattoo comes in. Do less, do bigger, do better is a simple but critical concept.

My rough benchmark is having no more than five jobs to be done; five things to focus on delivering with pace and excellence.

What's brilliantly ironic about doing less is that it allows you to… do more in the long run. You do something small, do it well, iron out the kinks, and figure out how to scale it or learn that it's not for you and stop it sooner.

You can show success and impact much more quickly if you do fewer things.

One great example is from my India team. A lean team with lean budgets, instead of trying to launch our new 'Pearson Test of English' campaign to the whole country, we decided to focus on Punjab and Haryana.

Having that focus meant we could afford a whole 360-degree campaign built on meaningful regional insights. It meant we had the time and budget to succeed, allowing us to refine an approach that can now be scaled across the rest of India and other markets.

Resisting temptation

Though 'do less, do bigger, do better' appeals to many on paper, people struggle to stick to it in practice.

What starts as a handful of neat priorities, gradually blooms into a whole shopping list as new things creep in or new business challenges take hold.

That's not to say priorities can't change. If the last few years have taught us anything, it's to expect the unexpected.

But when new opportunities present themselves, it's about going back to that list of five and deciding whether to deprioritize something else or to file the shiny new opportunity away under 'great idea, not right now'.

Do less, do bigger, do better

Chapter 5 of Jim Collins' book *Good to Great* is all about the Hedgehog Concept.

Named after a parable, there's a cunning fox with many strategies for catching the hedgehog and a hedgehog with one simple strategy to avoid becoming dinner: roll up into a really spiky, hard-to-eat ball.

Spiky ball wins. Having one focused approach wins.

Ditch the priorities shopping list and come and join me on Team Hedgehog. Forehead tattoo optional.

The importance of asking questions 16

So far we have focused on understanding and analysing our digital branding by building an actionable dashboard. In order to bridge gaps in our data we have discussed taking sample data and keeping things as simple as possible. Although this is a very practical and hands-on approach, we need to make sure that it is accurate and reflects the actual impact our digital branding is having on our business objective.

The final step we can take to check this is to question those people who have already completed the final step in our business objectives and understand what different experiences shaped their impression of us, influenced their behaviour and led them to complete our business objective.

Confirming not predicting

Figure 16.1 shows how we can work in the opposite direction to when we use a dashboard: rather than predicting what the outcome will be, we start with the outcome and see how the online/offline experiences have impacted this.

This allows us to confirm what impact each of our marketing activities has had on achieving our business objective, and we can do this by simply asking some questions. The questions we need to ask are not opinion-based but simply a list of tick boxes asking what experiences people had before they completed the final step. Then, by running this multiple times, we can start to get a picture of how important each of these experiences are.

Sum of experiences

In order to ask the correct questions I need an exhaustive list of the different potential touchpoints/experiences of my customer. These could include

Figure 16.1 Working in the opposite direction to a dashboard and understanding the contribution of each channel

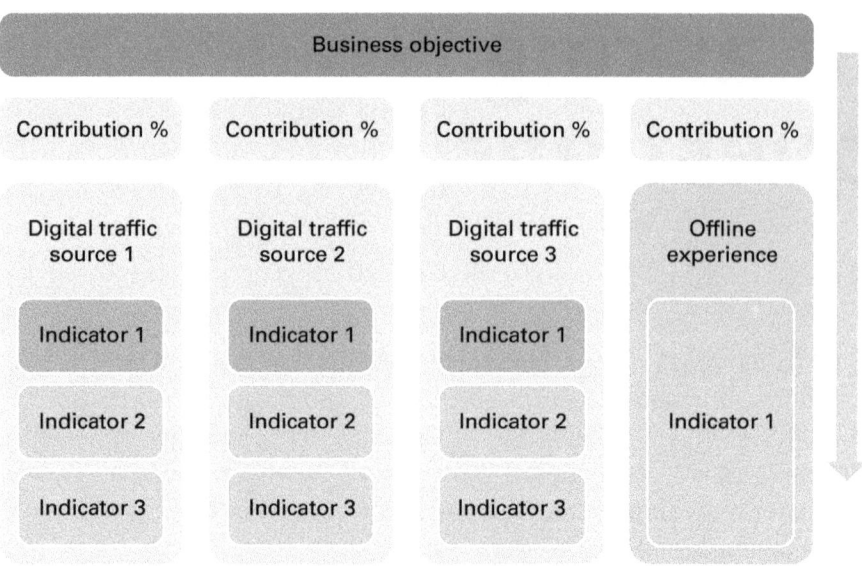

online and offline marketing activities, customer services encounters, events and word-of-mouth recommendations. Once I have asked which of these experiences happened before the final objective was completed, I can then see what percentage of journeys that end in a business objective involved this experience. This is very much like the percentages we use when looking at multichannel funnels in Google Analytics.

The sum of the percentages will normally add up to more than 100 per cent, as there will be a lot of overlap – but they will start to highlight for us which touchpoints are involved in the majority of objective completions.

Checking my dashboard

By carrying out this exercise and looking at how much each touchpoint has been involved in achieving my business objective, I can potentially go back and check what my dashboard is telling me. This means that any assumptions or mistakes made in the dashboard can be identified and removed. This may mean changing the primaries that I am monitoring or looking again at my gap correlation.

This iterative approach means that not only are we optimizing our digital branding via dashboards, but we are refining the dashboards and feeding back from actual business results.

No one said it was going to be easy

Sampling data during the dashboard process and sampling from final results to refine this process may seem complex. However, in reality it is a fairly straightforward thing to do, but it needs to be built into your day-to-day business practice in order to minimize the effort needed to collect the data. Your call centre, customer service and event staff should be trained and familiar with collecting the appropriate data as part of their normal roles. Your offline ads should be orientated towards driving a feedback mechanism of some type.

> **DASHBOARDS AND SURVEYING TEMPLATES**
>
> Don't forget, we have produced a dashboard framework that you can download in full and adjust to your own requirements to help track and improve your digital branding efforts, with special fields for using surveying to help assess activity. We've included a space in this for double checking your assumptions:
>
> http://www.targetinternet.com/digitalbranding.

Conclusions

We have looked at digital branding as the sum of all experiences we have with a brand and we've tried to put together a process that much more clearly allows us to measure the impact of each of these experiences. Although there is no perfect process for trying to work out what motivates human beings to act the way they do, we can come a lot closer to understanding how each part of digital branding is contributing to the whole.

For too long, agencies and brands themselves have implemented marketing that has very little correlation to what the business objective is and how this will impact the bottom line in the long or short term. I am not arguing against innovative and creative campaigns that may not always work. In fact, I actively encourage you to take some risks and try things out. However, I suggest doing this within a framework of measurement so we can clearly see what is working and what isn't and work out where to make adjustments.

Improve the branding and improve the process

As well as trying to have a clear view on why we are carrying out a particular marketing activity, within a measurement framework that allows us to see its contribution to our objectives, we also need to be open to improving the process. What I mean is that there is no one solution, measurement framework or dashboard that will suit every situation. We should therefore try to implement the methodologies outlined in this book but also be open to adjusting and improving them as we learn from the process.

The data science of branding

Data science is essentially about dealing with large amounts of information, trying to make sense of it and drawing sensible conclusions. That is fundamentally what digital branding is all about: bringing together lots of information and understanding how the sum of small pieces make up the whole.

As technology integration improves, this becomes much easier. One of the key challenges we face is that of integrating our sources of information, building a single customer view and making smarter analysis of this information. What we are trying to do with the process outlined in the measurement section of this book is to fix the gaps that currently exist in our systems and technology.

AI, data and branding

Throughout this book we have been looking at the various ways in which artificial intelligence (AI) can assist our digital branding efforts, as well as how we can orientate the risks they pose. A final opportunity, and a very significant one, is the advance data analysis that many generative AI platforms can help us carry out. By providing accurate data, AI can now carry out analysis and even create predictive models very easily, without the need for data science or coding experience. This leap forward in the ability to carry out detailed analysis so easily is one that can create great competitive advantage and is currently hugely underutilized, so is well worth the investment in upskilling and experimentation.

The sum of all experiences

Let's go back to the point that digital branding is about the sum of all experiences we have of something – and the impact this has. We should be able to see that by measuring more closely how each of these experiences work together to achieve our desired outcomes.

Digital branding is all about making smarter decisions based on facts and less on assumption.

REFERENCES AND FURTHER READING

Part One

GWI (2024) The Second-Screening Trends to Know, https://www.gwi.com/reports/second-screening-infographic (archived at https://perma.cc/984L-FTXV)

Chapter 1: What digital branding really means

AMA (2024) Definitions of Marketing, https://www.ama.org/the-definition-of-marketing-what-is-marketing/ (archived at https://perma.cc/Q6GM-7WCU)

Dörner, K and Edelman, D (2015) What 'Digital' Really Means, *McKinsey & Co*, https://www.mckinsey.com/industries/technology-media-and-telecommunications/our-insights/what-digital-really-means (archived at https://perma.cc/4QFY-94ZQ)

Huang, G (2010) How to Start a Movement? Leadership Lessons from Dancing Guy, *YouTube.com*, https://www.youtube.com/watch?v=lbaemWIljeQc (archived at https://perma.cc/MD2Y-A992)

Chapter 3: Considering the user journey

Think with Google (2017) Micro-Moments, https://www.thinkwithgoogle.com/marketing-strategies/micro-moments/ (archived at https://perma.cc/T8LR-QJMG)

Chapter 4: Objectives and authenticity

The Impact of Marketing Part 2 (2021) *Digital Vision: Living on the Cutting Edge*, The Chartered Institute of Marketing, UK, https://my.cim.co.uk/media/73349/cim-impact-of-marketing-report-part-2.pdf (archived at https://perma.cc/39NC-AZBJ)

Chapter 5: Social media

CMO Survey UK (2021) *UK Topline Report*, Leadership Institute, London Business School, London, https://cmosurvey.org/wp-content/uploads/2021/02/The_CMO_Survey-Topline_Report-February-2021_UK.pdf (archived at https://perma.cc/9A49-HPDZ)

Macready, H (2024) How Often to Post to Social Media in 2024, *Hootsuite Social Media Marketing & Management Dashboard*, https://blog.hootsuite.com/how-often-to-post-on-social-media/ (archived at https://perma.cc/3XM4-RN6H)

Thales (2024) Trust in Social Media, https://cpl.thalesgroup.com/digital-trust-index (archived at https://perma.cc/H4EJ-KEXR)

WebFX (2024) Twitter Mobile Users, https://www.webfx.com/blog/social-media/why-twitter-matters-to-marketing-infographic/ (archived at https://perma.cc/8DBS-XVVY)

YouGov (2016) YouGov: HP Facebook, USA, https://d25d2506sfb94s.cloudfront.net/cumulus_uploads/document/lcergepzz1/tabs_HP_Facebook_20160425.pdf (archived at https://perma.cc/92RS-7VXU)

6Sense (2024) Google Analytics Market Share, https://6sense.com/tech/dashboard/google-analytics-market-share (archived at https://perma.cc/G6DN-T9VS)

Chapter 6: Search

Campaign (2007) Cadbury 'Gorilla' Wins Campaign of the Year, http://www.campaignlive.co.uk/features/773064/ (archived at https://perma.cc/4YBD-Z7BY)

SEMRush (2024) 34 Eye-Opening Google Search Statistics for 2024, https://www.semrush.com/blog/google-search-statistics/ (archived at https://perma.cc/QGC8-W4HB)

Chapter 7: Mobile

Chaffey, D (2024) 2024 Mobile Marketing Statistics Compilation, *Smart Insights*, https://www.smartinsights.com/mobile-marketing/mobile-marketing-analytics/mobile-marketing-statistics/ (archived at https://perma.cc/XEV7-VPU2)

CNBC.com (2021) TECH Apple's App Store Had Gross Sales around $64 Billion Last Year and It's Growing Strongly Again, *CNBC*, https://www.cnbc.com/2021/01/08/apples-app-store-had-gross-sales-around-64-billion-in-2020.html (archived at https://perma.cc/QDB8-VXLE)

Donnelly, G (2021) Are You Ready for Mobile-First Indexing? 5 Things to Check Now, *Wordstream.com*, https://www.wordstream.com/blog/ws/2021/04/15/mobile-first-indexing (archived at https://perma.cc/XR6E-QPLK)

Hewitt, M (2017) How to Ensure You Are Ready for the Mobile-first SERP, *Stickyeyes*, https://www.stickyeyes.com/2017/02/24/five-ways-to-ensure-that-you-are-ready-for-the-mobile-first-serp/ (archived at https://perma.cc/9DXK-4MTV)

Titcomb, J (2016) Mobile Web Usage Overtakes Desktop for First Time, *The Telegraph*, http://www.telegraph.co.uk/technology/2016/11/01/mobile-web-usage-overtakes-desktop-for-first-time/ (archived at https://perma.cc/KY6G-GGU4)

Chapter 9: Email marketing

MailButler (2024) Email Mobile Stats, https://www.mailbutler.io/blog/email/email-statistics-trends/ (archived at https://perma.cc/NXL4-BCSP)

MailChimp (2017) Effects of List Segmentation on Email Marketing Stats, http://mailchimp.com/resources/research/effects-of-list-segmentation-on-email-marketing-stats/ (archived at https://perma.cc/LJL7-EC82)

Chapter 12: Measuring digital branding

Kicksta (2024) How to Identify Fake Instagram Followers & Put a Stop to Them, https://blog.kicksta.co/how-to-identify-fake-instagram-followers-put-a-stop-to-them/ (archived at https://perma.cc/E84B-BKYJ)

Chapter 14: The role of analytics

Alphabet Investor Relations (2024) https://abc.xyz/investor/index.html (archived at https://perma.cc/TKM8-Q9LA)

W^{3}Techs (2024) Market Share Trends for Traffic Analysis Tools, https://w3techs.com/technologies/history_overview/traffic_analysis (archived at https://perma.cc/T2QL-VPUE)

INDEX

Note: Page numbers in *italics* refer to tables or figures.

Ad Rank 102
advocates 70, 71
AdWords 101–02, 103, 121
algorithms 76, 95
analytics 59–60
API (application programming interface) 155
Apple 109–10, 144–45, 175
   email design 137–39
Apple TV 109–10
artificial intelligence (AI) 1, 47, 106, 127–28, *128*, 146, 167, 211
   CRM and 156–57
   deepfakes 1, 8, 48
   risks and ethical challenges 8–9
Attention, Interest, Desire, Action framework 34
authenticity 43–48
   authentic value proposition 46–47
   branding for differentiation 44–45
   deepfakes 1, 8, 48
   Pepsi Refresh Project 44, 45

BACN 128
Baidu 75, 80, 87, 100
BigQuery 119, 120
Bill 120–21
Bing 75, 81, 87
'brand awareness'
   as an excuse 4–5
   term 1
brand building' 115
brand democracy 8
brand experience 7
brand image 7
brand metrics, traditional 10–11
branding, data science of 210–11
branding, traditional view of 3–4, 7
British Telecom 48
business objectives 16–17, *17*
Business to business (B2B) 9, 18, 27–28, 30, 49, 52
business to consumer (B2C) 5, 28–29
Butler, Gemma 46–47

Cadbury 78–79, *79*, *80*
California 176

California Consumer Privacy Act (CCPA) 144
Cambridge Analytica scandal 144
CAN-SPAM Act 146, 148
Catholic Church 42
charity funding 19
Chartered Institute of Marketing 5
ChatGPT 48, 52, 106, 127
China, social media in 59
click-through rate (CTR) 102, 116, 119, 136
   sending and testing 141–42, *142*
CMO Survey UK 67
Coca-Cola 44
complex consumer products 19
consumer packaged goods (CPG) 18–19
content and narratives 24–25
content management system (CMS) 88, 93, 111, 187
content mapping 33, *33*
content marketing 30–31, *30*, *31*
conversational customer journey 67–68
cookies
   in digital marketing 175
   first-party data 175–76
   privacy regulations and consumer attitudes 176
Core Web Vitals 83
cost per mille (CPM) 116
CPC/CPA (cost per click/ cost per acquisition) 100–01
culture and process 61–62, *62*
customer relationship management (CRM) 123, 124, 127, 135–36, 143
   and AI chatbots 156–57
   automation systems 158–61
   CRM and ESP integration 154–56, *156*
   definitions and practicalities 151–52
   digital branding dashboards 184
   marketing automation 157–58, *158*
   marketing automation, warning on 162
   personalization and triggering 157
   single customer view and data 152–54, *153*
   testing, learning and adjusting 161–62

Davids, Jon 35–42
Dawley, Sarah 67–68

Index

deepfakes 1, 8, 48
digital branding, measuring
   brand value, defining 173
   cookies 175–76
   different measurement techniques 179–81, *180*
   marketing activity, value of 173–74
   social measures, benchmarked 177–79
digital branding, view of 3–5
   traditional view of 3–4, 7
Digital Marketing Podcast 8
digital transformation, role of 12–15
digital transformer, tips for 13–15
Dörner, Karel 13
'drumming gorilla ad' 78, *79*, 80
due diligence 62–63

Edelman, David 13
EEAT guidelines 83–84
Eleven Labs 8, 52
email marketing
   AI tools and 127–28, *128*
   core principles of 125–27, *126*
   dynamic content generation and rules 142–43
   email and user journey 129–30
   email design 137–39
   email list 135–36
   email list, collecting 133–35
   email service provider 132–33
   email templates 139–41, *140*
   'last click' perspective 130–32, *131*
   open rates and click-through rates 136–37
   privacy 144
   relevance, focusing on 129
   sending and testing 141–42, *142*
email regulations (CAN-SPAM) 138
email service provider (ESP) 124, 127, 132–33
   CRM and ESP integration 154–56, *156*
   definitions and practicalities 151–52
   dynamic content generation and rules 142–43
   email list 135–36
   email list, collecting 133–35
   email templates 139–41, *140*
   open rates and click-through rates 136–37
   personalization and triggering 157
   privacy 144
   sending and testing 141–42, *142*
EU 146
Europe 144, 176
Exton, Rachel 204–06

Facebook 49–50, 53, 68, 76, 105–06, 123, 145, 177, 178, 179, 203
Facebook Insights 57
'frictionless technology' 110

Gap correlation 198–99
   offline channels and experiences 200–01, *200*
   offline indicators 201–03, *202*
GDPR legislation 144, 146, 148, 176
Gemini 52, 127
generative AI and content 52–53
Gmail 128
goals and conversions 35
Goldman Sachs 48
Google 50, 75, 81, 109, 111, 118, 130, 144, 174
   algorithms 76
   core reports 188–94, *192*
   EEAT guidelines 83–84
   email design 137–39
   paid search 97–101, *98*
   setting up analytics 187–88
   user behaviour 94–95
   webmaster guidelines 92
   see also SEO (search engine optimization)
Google Ads 99, 190
Google Adwords 101–02, 103, 121
Google Analytics 59–60, 99, 119, 124, 130, 132, 182, 199, 208
Google Analytics 4 (GA4) 99, 185–87, 188
   core reports 188–94, *192*
Google Business Profile 87, *87*
Google Data Studio 120
Google operators 82
Google Search Console 82
Google Tag Manager 187
Google Trends 54–56, *55*, 78, *79*, 86–87, *88*
'Google URL builder' 195
Google+ 178
GWI 4

Haryana 205
Hootsuite 67–68
HTC 109

influence, judging 73
influencers 72, 73
Instagram 4–5, 53, 68, 105–06, 181
integration
   multichannel marketing 164–65
   omni-channel marketing 165–66
   self-optimizing campaigns 167
Internet Advertising Bureau (IAB) 117
iPad 109–10

iPhone 109–10
iPod 109–10

Kaushik, Avinash 33
ketogenic diet 39–40
KPIs 14

'last click' approach 182–84, *183*, *184*, 194
link authority, measuring 95, 96
link building 93–94
Link Explorer 95–96, *96*
LinkedIn 27, 43, 53
luxury brands 19–20

MacDonald, Jonathan 8
MailChimp 133
mobile marketing
    AI 106
    apps 113–14
    fundamentals 111–13, *112*
    integrated devices 107–08
    local-based consumer 107
    mobile optimization 108
    mobile sites and responsive design 110–11
    technology challenges 109–10
    technology, sake of 105–06
    user journey 106–07, *107*
Movement Formula 35–42, *37*
Moz 95–96, *96*
multichannel marketing 26

Nike 76

'Off on a Digital Journey' course 13–15
online advertising
    Ad networks vs. media owners 117–18
    Ad reporting and analytics 119–20
    ad targeting, types of 118–19
    creative options 119
    objectives 116–17
on-page optimization 88–93, *90*
    alt text 93
    copy 92
    file names 92
    headings 91
    link text 92
    page title 89–90
    users first, then search engines 89
    web page names 91
Open Handset Alliance (OHA) 109
OpenAI 48
organized religion 41–42

paid search 97–101, *98*
Pearson 204–06
Pepsi 44, 45

Pepsi Refresh Project 44, 45
PPC (pay per click) 78, 79, 80, 86, 97–103, *98*, 121–24
    additional ad features 100
    considerations 101–03
    conversion tracking 102
    create ad copy 99–100
    fundamentals 98
    keyword research 99
    ongoing management and optimization 101
    quality scoring and ad rank 101–02
    set budgets and bids 100–01
    set objectives 99
    set targeting criteria 100
    working with PPC agencies 102–03
PPC/SEO relationship 80, 103–04
public relations (PR) 73–74
Punjab 205

questions
    dashboard 208–09
    experiences, sum of 207–08, *208*

real-world integration 60
Responsive design 108
return on investment (ROI) 1, 2, 121, 129, 170, 176, 179
Rogers, Ciaran 120–24

Safari web browser 144
sales funnel, traditional 31–32, *32*
Samsung 109
search 78–104
    'drumming gorilla ad' 78, 79, 80
    link building 93–94
    on-page optimization 88–93, *90*
    PPC/SEO relationship 80
    search engine algorithms 95
    SEO (search engine optimization) 79, 81–83 PPC 79, 97–103, *98*
Search Console 190
search engine marketing (SEM) 79
See, Think, Do, Care framework *32*, 33, 34–35
sentiment analysis 74–75
SEO (search engine optimization) 73–74, 78, 79, 81–83, 96–97
    AI content and 83–84
    ethical SEO 92
    generic search terms 85
    keyword research for 84–88
    link building 93–94
    local search 87, *87*
    long tail search 85–86
    mobile search 81
    on-page optimization 88–93, *90*

Index

Smart Insights 107
social listening 56, 64, 65
social measurement 74
social media 51–77
    content and engagement 52
    culture and process 61–62, *62*
    generative AI and content 52–53
    informing your social media approach 54–56
    mobile social media experience 53
    monitoring and listening tools 56–58, *58*
    social as personal 51
    social listening 56
    social media policy 60–61, *60*, *61*, *63*, 70–71
    user journey and value proposition 52
    using search to inform content themes 54–56, *55*
    see also social media crisis management plan; social media disasters
social media advertising 75–76
    algorithms, trusting 76
    paid search 97–101, *98*
    value proposition, privacy and trust 75
Social Media Benchmark 5
social media crisis management plan 69–71
    holding patterns 70
    monitoring reaction 70
    not responding 69
    post-crisis debrief and social policy update 70–71
    speed of response 69
social media disasters 10, *60*, *61*, 62–69
    clear responsibilities 65–66, *66*
    crisis management team 69
    disaster prediction 64
    escalation process 68
    ongoing monitoring 65
    panel sign off 62–63
    response tracking 67
    social listening 56, 64, 65
    social media crisis management plan 69–71
    social media policy 60–61, *60*, *61*, 63
    staff training 65
social media engagement 71, 72
social media outreach 71, 72
social media policy 60–61, *60*, *61*, 63, 70–71

social signals 94
Sony 109
SparkToro.com 57, *58*, 73
Steve 120–21
sustainable marketing 46–47
'sustainable transformation' 46–47

target audience objectives 16–17, *17*
TargetInternet.com 33, *33*, 48
Tesco.com 33, *33*
TikTok 59
touchpoints, clarification 11–12
transmedia storytelling 166
TripAdvisor 3

UK House of Commons 48
Universal Analytics (UA) 186
Upfluence 72, 73, 94
UpWork.com 139
user behaviour 94–95
user journey 20–24, 26–29
    business to business example 27–28
    business to consumer example 28–29
    examples 26–29
    mapping 34–35
    stages of 31–33
UTM 122

value investing 40–41
value proposition 17, 30, 34

web analytics
    attribution modelling 194–95
    core reports 188–94, *192*
    dashboards and analytics 196, *196*
    Google Analytics 4 (GA4) 185–87, 188
    'last click' approach 182–84, *183*, *184*
    setting up analytics 187–88
    tracking code 195
Welham, Alistair 12–15
WhatsApp 53
WordPress 91

X 27, 178, 181

Yahoo 87
Yale Climate Connections 42
YouTube 10, 53, 59, 78

Looking for another book?

Explore our award-winning books from global business experts in Marketing and Sales

Scan the code to browse

www.koganpage.com/marketing

More from Kogan Page

ISBN: 9781398609792

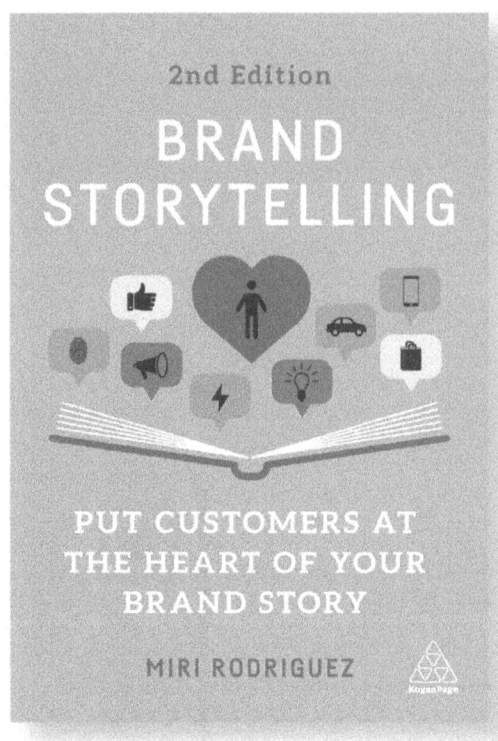

ISBN: 9781398610088

www.koganpage.com

EU Representative (GPSR)

Authorised Rep Compliance Ltd, Ground Floor, 71 Lower Baggot Street, Dublin, D02 P593, Ireland

www.arccompliance.com

www.ingramcontent.com/pod-product-compliance
Lightning Source LLC
Chambersburg PA
CBHW042005141125
35353CB00061B/759